ISLAM
A First Encounter

Kent P. Jackson

THE JERUSALEM CENTER
FOR NEAR EASTERN STUDIES
Brigham Young University

Published by the Jerusalem Center for Near Eastern Studies, Brigham Young University, Provo, Utah, USA.

Printed in the United States of America by Sheridan Books, Inc.

Cover and interior design by Emily V. Strong.

ISBN: 978-1-9443-9479-0

Contents

Contents

Introduction

What Is Islam?

Terms and Names to Know

Middle East, Near East, South Asia, Islam, Muslim, Arab, Allah, prophet, Muhammad, Qur'an

This book, intentionally very short and simple, is a first encounter. My desire in these pages is to introduce Islam to non-Muslim readers so they can know enough to do two things: (1) have knowledgeable and respectful conversations with Muslims whenever they meet them and (2) be well informed when they watch or read news reports that involve Islam or Muslims. Because this book is short, be forewarned that every chapter in it deals with subjects worthy of many volumes, and indeed many good volumes have been written on every topic in it. I am not a Muslim myself, but I have taught Islam to non-Muslim university students (and many Muslims as well) for many years. I have Muslim friends, I have lived and worked among Muslims, and I have traveled extensively in Muslim-majority lands. I am an admiring friend of Muslims, their rich and fascinating culture, and the religious principles that influence their lives in positive ways.

Because the intent of this book is neither to proselytize nor to criticize, it generally just tells the story. As readers would likely want others to treat their own beliefs, this book will present the history without the use of words like *claimed* or *alleged* every time something involving the divine is discussed. Often this practice involves discussing events and explaining matters as believers do themselves. Studying someone else's religion is an opportunity to learn things about one's own beliefs, but that comes when readers seek not only to understand but also to notice aspects of the religion that are worthy of their respect.

This book will be more descriptive than analytical, meaning that it will often answer questions like what and how rather than why. Although we will look at the lives and contributions of famous and important people, there will be special emphasis on what ordinary Muslims believe and do.

Countries with Largest Muslim Populations
(worldatlas.com, 2018)

1. Indonesia, 227 million
2. Pakistan, 204 million
3. India, 189 million
4. Bangladesh, 149 million
5. Nigeria, 95 million
6. Egypt, 87 million
7. Iran, 82 million
8. Turkey, 81 million

Definitions

To introduce the topic, we first need to examine some terms that readers will see from time to time. First, *Middle East* and *Near East*. Generally, these terms refer to the area from Egypt to Iran (west to east) and from Turkey to Yemen (north to south). The term *Near East* is used more in the context of the ancient world, while *Middle East* is used more for the medieval and modern world. Sometimes the countries of North Africa (Morocco to Libya) and Afghanistan and Pakistan are included under the term *Middle East*, or *Middle East and North Africa*. In discussions of Islam, the geographical designation *South Asia* is seen frequently. Generally speaking, this term is used with reference to the countries from Afghanistan in the west to Indonesia in the east.

The term *Islam* refers to the religion discussed in this book. A *Muslim* is one who adheres to that religion. *Muslim* is only a religious designation and tells us nothing about ethnicity, language, location, nationality, or political views.

An *Arab* is someone whose native language is Arabic, so the term does not tell us anything about a person's religion or political views. Some readers may assume that all Arabs are Muslims, or that all the people in the Middle East are Muslims. Such is not the case. The Middle East is the birthplace not only of Islam but also of Judaism and Christianity. Millions of Christians live in the Middle East, and there are sizable Christian minorities in most Arab countries. Egypt, for example, has about seven or eight million Arab Christian citizens.

Muslims can be found in many nations and among many ethnic groups. In the list above, we see that of the eight countries in the world with the highest Muslim populations, only Egypt, Iran, and Turkey are in the Middle East. Egypt is the only Arab country on the list, because although Iran and Turkey are Middle Eastern countries, Iranians and Turks are not Arabs. Indonesia, the country with the highest Muslim population in the world, is three thousand miles away from the Middle East and the nearest Arab country.

What Is Islam?

Islam is a religion that began in Arabia in the seventh century CE and since then has spread to become a worldwide faith. Today there are about a billion and a half people in the world who identify themselves as Muslims.

The word *Islam* means "submission"—submission to God—and each believer is called a *Muslim*, "one who submits" to God. Muslims worship the same God that Christians and Jews worship—"the God of Abraham, the God of Isaac, and the God of Jacob" (Exodus 4:5), "the Compassionate, the Merciful" (Qur'an 1.1). The Arabic name of God, *Allah*, is the same word that is used in the Arabic New Testament for the Christian God (in John 3:16, for example).

Because Muslims are not a nationality or an ethnic group but a community of believers, they can be found among all races and in every nation. More than three million Muslims live in the United States, and their numbers continue to grow.

Muslims see Islam as the true religion since the beginning of time. They believe that God's will is made known by *prophets*, humans through whom God has delivered messages to his people. The last of those was Muhammad, who lived in Arabia in the sixth and seventh centuries. Muslims believe that through him, God revealed in Arabic the Qur'an, a collection of divine communications to guide believers from Muhammad's time to the present.

Many prophets preceded Muhammad. The Qur'an names earlier prophets, including many who are known from the Jewish and Christian scriptures, such as Adam, Abraham, and John the Baptist. Islam teaches that through the long history of God's dealings with humanity, he revealed true religion through all of his prophets. But inevitably, the people eventually strayed from prophetic teachings, and humankind entered into periods of confusion and ignorance until there was a restoration of truth through a new prophet. Some prophets were sent to one nation and others to other nations, and to some God revealed books. Notable among those were Moses, to whom God revealed a book called the *Tawra*, or Law/Teaching, and Jesus, to whom God revealed a book called the *Injil*, or Gospel. Muslims believe that later people changed those records, so despite their divine origins, the Old and New Testaments no longer contain God's

word in its purity. Jesus is not divine, but he is one of the foremost prophets in Islam.

The cycle of revelation, apostasy, and restoration continued through history until Muhammad, the last of the prophets. Through him, God gave the world his final and perfect revelation—the Qur'an.

That is the overview; the rest of the book fills in the details.

About This Book

The first chapters in this book discuss the early history and basic beliefs of Islam, followed by chapters that deal with Islam in the lives of ordinary people. In keeping with the objective of helping readers be informed consumers of the news, chapters will then deal with topics relevant to political

The al-Farooq Mosque in Atlanta, Georgia, USA, is evidence that Islam is a worldwide religion. This mosque serves a growing Muslim community and operates a school and a cemetery for Muslim burials.

Islam. The final chapters will survey the story of Muslims in Europe and North America.

The pictures in this book are not decorative but display people and things that are integral to the story of Islam. Coming from over a dozen countries, including from countries that do not have Muslim majorities, they illustrate how widespread Islam is but also how diverse it is. The images and their explanations often contain information that is not included in the text but that is important for understanding the subject matter of the chapters as well as for seeing Islam's impact on the lives of believers. They also show that Islam is, among other things, a religion that is visually interesting.

Because this is a short and introductory book written for a broad audience, it does not contain notes and references that would be appropriate in a more academic work. For the same reason, the transliterated words have been kept simple and do not contain diacritical marks, except in the word *Qur'an*. Transliterated Arabic words are generally italicized, but those that are making their way into English usage (such as *imam* and *muezzin*) are not.

The Qur'an has been translated frequently into modern languages. Unless noted otherwise, the English translation used in this book is that of M. A. S. Abdel Haleem, *The Qur'an: English Translation and Parallel Arabic Text* (New York: Oxford University Press, 2016). Citations in parentheses include the chapter and verse numbers, for example, "(85.21)." For other passages I have preferred the translation in Seyyed Hossein Nasr, et al., *The Study Quran: A New Translation and Commentary* (New York: HarperCollins, 2015). These are noted with superscripted "N" after the verse number. Quotations from the *hadith* come from https://sunnah.com, sometimes with minor edits. Citations include the collection followed by the *hadith* number; for example, "(Bukhari 13)."

Where can readers learn more? Hopefully this book will be not only an encounter but also an invitation. As pointed out earlier, good sources abound for every topic, every Arabic word, every doctrine, every conflict, and every prominent person mentioned in these pages. If one turns to online bookstores, one can find a lot of material. In addition, the internet now conveniently provides much helpful and reliable information posted by Muslims themselves and also by knowledgeable non-Muslims.

Chapter 1

Muhammad

Terms and Names to Know

hadith, ibn Ishaq, Mecca, Khadija, Kaaba, Aisha, Medina, Hijra, Battle of Badr, Battle of the Trench, *umma*, Night Journey and Ascension, Seal of the Prophets, SAAS, SAWS, ﷺ, PBUH, *sunna*, Sunnis, Shia

Three major sources provide what is known of the life of Muhammad. The first of these is the Qur'an, a collection of revelations he received. The revelations did not all come at once but gradually over the course of about two decades. They are not dated, and in the printed Qur'an they are not arranged with chronological order in mind. Because they make repeated reference to Muhammad, they are an important source, though they are not intended to be biographical in any real way.

The second major source for Muhammad's life is what is called the *hadith* literature. Sometimes called "traditions," it is a vast collection of statements by those who knew the Prophet, put together in the centuries after his life. These statements recall what he said and did.

Our third source is a biography of Muhammad written by a Muslim named ibn Ishaq. Ibn Ishaq apparently drafted it over a century after Muhammad's death, but the final form we have dates to about a century later. It is based on what was known of the Prophet's life in the decades after his time. Most Muslims accept its biographical information as transmitted accurately and as a faithful account of his life. Modern historians may be less certain of some of the details, but they use its story as the starting point for putting together a narrative of Muhammad's career. In the centuries after ibn Ishaq, other historians also wrote about Muhammad and his times.

Prophet

Muhammad was born in the Arabian city of Mecca around 570 CE, of the Hashemite family of Mecca's Quraysh tribe. He was orphaned early in life and was raised by an uncle. Most Muslims believe that Muhammad never learned to read and write, which is an important matter because it provides confirmation to them that the Qur'an, a written book, was a miracle and was not of his own creation.

Muhammad managed a caravan for a wealthy widowed merchant named Khadija. In about 595 he accepted her offer of marriage and became her husband. She was older than Muhammad and died around 620, but before then she would become his first convert and greatest supporter.

Muhammad's prophetic call came in about 610. Arabian society was polytheistic, and Mecca, the city where he and Khadija lived, had an economy based both on trade and on the fact that it was a religious center. In the city there was (and still is) a large cubical structure called the Kaaba, 13 x 13 x 11 meters in dimension, which housed images of the city's gods. Muslims believe that the Kaaba was built by Abraham and his son Ishmael, or repaired by them but built earlier by Adam. In Muhammad's time, annual pilgrimages to the Kaaba to worship Mecca's gods brought visitors and their money into the city.

Even before his call, Muhammad was sensitive to spiritual things and to the evils in the world around him. The materialism of Mecca bothered him deeply, as did its polytheism. To meditate, worship, and pray, he often went to a mountain outside the city, where he would find seclusion in a cave. The narrative that follows is that of Muhammad's later wife Aisha, from her account recorded in the *hadith* literature. She reported that Muhammad "used to go in seclusion in the cave of Hira, where he used to worship Allah continuously for many nights before going back to his family to take the necessary provision (of food) for the stay." On one occasion while he was worshipping in the cave, "an Angel came to him and asked him to read. Allah's Apostle replied, 'I do not know how to read.'" The verb translated here as "read" also means "recite." *Qur'an*, which means "Recitation," comes from the same root. Muhammad was terrified and had no words to proclaim.

> The Prophet (☪) added, "Then the Angel held me (forcibly) and pressed me so hard that I felt distressed. Then he released me and again asked me to read, and I replied, 'I do not know how to read.' Thereupon he held me again and

pressed me for the second time till I felt distressed. He then released me and asked me to read, but again I replied. 'I do not know how to read.' Thereupon he held me for the third time and pressed me till I got distressed, and then he released me and said, 'Recite in the name of your Lord who created—created man from clots of blood. Recite! Your Lord is the Most Bountiful One, who by the pen taught man what he did not know.'" (Bukhari 4953)

The words at the end are a passage in the Qur'an, the first revelation from God to Muhammad (96.1–5). Muhammad was terrified as he returned to Khadija, who provided him with comfort and encouragement. She took him to her uncle, who told him, "This is the same Angel (Gabriel) who was sent to Moses," thus connecting Muhammad's revelation with others from the past (Bukhari 4953). Revelation ceased for a while, but the Prophet later reported, "Once while I was walking, all of a sudden I heard a voice from the sky. I looked up and saw, to my surprise, the same Angel that had visited me in the cave of Hira. . . . I got afraid of him and came back home" (Bukhari 4954). In response, God told Muhammad, "You wrapped in your cloak, arise and give warning! Proclaim the greatness of your Lord; . . . do not weaken, feeling overwhelmed; be steadfast in your Lord's cause" (74.1–3, 6–7).

As Muhammad understood and embraced his calling, revelations came as needed to guide him and his followers. His earliest converts were family members and close friends, but over the course of time others came to believe his message, and eventually a sizable body of Muslims was found in Mecca.

Muhammad's new religion was a problem for the leaders of Mecca. The revelations were the words of one god, Allah, and they condemned the very existence of any other gods. This monotheistic message was an economic threat to the Meccans, because if it spread widely it would cut into the income that resulted from the pilgrimages to worship the various deities. Over the course of time, persecution from the Meccan leaders against the growing Muslim community made it necessary for Muhammad and his followers to move to a new home.

In 622 the citizens of Yathrib, about 340 kilometers from Mecca, invited Muhammad to assume the leadership of their city. In response, he and the Muslims emigrated from Mecca to Yathrib, where he lived for the rest of his life. The city later became known as Medina. The relocation of the Muslim community to Medina is called the *Hijra*, "emigration," and it marks a turning point in the history of Islam. The new setting allowed the Muslims to worship safely and securely, and it marked the creation of an Islamic state. Muhammad was now not only a religious leader but also the political leader of Medina, and his influence then began to spread even farther. The Hijra is so important in Islamic history that the Muslim calendar begins with year 1 AH ("after Hijra") in 622 CE.

Opposition from the Meccans continued, because they now viewed the Muslims as a political threat. Battles between the two groups marked the next few years. In 624 the Battle of Badr took place, in which the Muslims conducted a successful raid against a Meccan caravan. Their victory proved to the Muslims that God was on their side. In 627 a large Meccan army attacked the Muslims at Medina. The Muslims dug a trench to protect their city, and they were able to defeat the Meccan army. The Battle of the Trench became a second victory in battle to convince the Muslims of the righteousness of their cause.

Finally, in 630 the Meccans conceded defeat. Muhammad and his followers took control of Mecca, cleansed the Kaaba of all the idols it contained, and rededicated it to the worship of Allah,

Surrounded by Mecca's Great Mosque is the Kaaba, the ancient cube-shaped structure that Muslims believe was built by Abraham. Once a temple to many gods, it was purified by Muhammad and is now the point of direction for Muslim prayers from everywhere in the world.

the one true God. An important word in Islam is *umma*, which we can translate conveniently as the "Muslim community"—not a place but the collective body of believers. Today the *umma* spreads across the world, but in Muhammad's lifetime it consisted mostly of his Arabian followers. During the remainder of his life, Muhammad's influence in Arabia grew, and through military conquest, alliances with various tribes, and religious conversion, by the time of his death he was the ruler of most of the Arabian Peninsula.

Seal of the Prophets

In the years when Muhammad lived in Mecca and Medina, he received the revelations that would eventually comprise the Qur'an. He had other prophetic experiences as well. Among the most significant was his Night Journey and Ascension, during which he traveled in one night from Mecca to "the Farthest Mosque"—traditionally interpreted as Jerusalem—and from there up to the presence of God. On the way he communicated with previous prophets and was shown a vision of hell. The Night Journey and Ascension, only touched on in the Qur'an but described in more detail in later tradition, has been seen by Muslims as either a physical relocation or a spiritual journey. Either way, it showed Muslims that Muhammad was a peer of the earlier great prophets. In later centuries, when Jerusalem became identified with the location of "the Farthest (al-Aqsa) Mosque," it was acknowledged as Islam's third holiest place. Mecca, the location of the Kaaba, is the most holy city to Muslims, and Medina, site of the first Islamic government and place of Muhammad's burial, is considered the second most sacred place.

In the last years of the Prophet's life, after the death of Khadija, he married multiple wives, including one named Aisha. She is often described as his favorite wife. She lived for about forty years after Muhammad's death, and she continued to be an important and influential member of the Muslim community.

Muhammad died in 632, but his religion did not die with him. Instead, its greatest growth took place soon after his death as his message and legacy spread. Muhammad is called the Seal of the Prophets (33.40), which Muslims have generally understood to mean the last prophet, the one who closes the book of prophecy and seals it. There will be no prophets or revelation after him.

Even though Muslims hold Muhammad in the highest regard, he is not to be considered divine or anything but a mortal man. Thus the older term *Mohammadan*, suggesting that the religion is about him, is both inaccurate and offensive. Only Allah is to be worshipped. Even so, Muslims are to speak of Muhammad with great respect. The Qur'an teaches: "Truly God and His angels invoke blessings upon the Prophet. O you who believe! Invoke blessings upon him, and greetings of peace!" (33.56^N). Every time Muhammad's name is mentioned, pious Muslims follow this injunction by blessing their Prophet's name, saying, in English translation, "May Allah bless him and grant him salvation." In written form, this is most often abbreviated with the letters "SAAS" or "SAWS" following his name, or printed in tiny Arabic calligraphy, "ﷺ." For other prophets, most Muslims say "Peace be upon him," abbreviated "PBUH," though some use "PBUH" for Muhammad as well.

Written here in Arabic calligraphy, the phrase "May Allah bless him and grant him salvation" is a customary invocation that one says or writes after mentioning Muhammad.

Muhammad's Night Journey and Ascension. Many Muslims have believed that it is never appropriate to make images of the Prophet. Exceptions like this one are found not in religious contexts but only in illustrated literary works. The covering of the Prophet's face with a veil is a common convention to preserve his unique standing. There are also images in which he is depicted unveiled, but they are not common. The nimbus, the flaming halo that emanates from the Prophet and also from his guide, the angel Gabriel, is found in almost all images of Muhammad. As described in traditions relating to the Night Journey and Ascension, Muhammad is mounted on his human-headed steed, Buraq, and he is surrounded by angels.

Artistic conventions like these show the reverence with which Muslims throughout history have treated Muhammad. Although he is never to be considered divine, Muslims view him as sinless and as the bearer of a holy mission, and thus the veiling and the surrounding flames set him visually apart from others. From a sixteenth-century manuscript from Persia, British Library, London.

Sunna and Hadith

In Islam, all prophets are important. Muhammad has a special role as the prophet of the final revelation, and thus he is worthy of the greatest admiration and emulation. Muslims consider his *sunna*—his "customary behavior," "usual practice," "way of acting"—to be the pattern of behavior that all should follow. Because of that, every remembered word and deed of his is important.

As mentioned earlier, a *hadith* is a report of something Muhammad said or did. These reports are important because they are the means by which the Prophet's *sunna* was preserved and transmitted. In Islam there are no prophets since Muhammad, and today there is no universally accepted central authority to guide the *umma*. In this Islam differs from most religious movements, including many Christian churches. There is authority, however, first in the Qur'an, which contains God's words, and second in Muhammad's *sunna* as found in the *hadith*, preserving his behaviors and sayings.

After Muhammad's death, accounts of his words and deeds circulated orally, and in time they were collected and recorded in written form. In order to preserve only authentic traditions, scholars investigated and evaluated every purported recollection for legitimacy and accuracy. That process lasted about 250 years. To be considered accurate, a *hadith* needed to have a reliable chain of transmission all the way back to an eyewitness in Muhammad's time. That chain of human transmission would go something like this: "A tells that B reported that C said that D heard the following from the Prophet (SAAS)." These provide the equivalent of a modern footnote to let the reader know the source. Muhammad's wife Aisha is a source for many of the *hadith*, along with other early Muslims.

There is no official collection of *hadith*, but some collections are very highly prized. Bukhari (died 870; 7400 *hadith*), Muslim (died 875; 3000 *hadith*), and al-Tirmidhi (died 892; 4000 *hadith*) are among those who produced collections that are widely respected today by Sunni Muslims, the majority Muslim group. Those men and others traveled all over the Muslim world and collected the sayings. Shia Muslims, the smaller of the two main Muslim groups, have other collections, though some of their *hadith* are the same as those in the Sunni collections.

Based on what we have seen so far, it is not surprising that some non-Muslim historians (and even some Muslims as well) have questioned the reliability of the *hadith* reports. Being collected over two centuries after the Prophet's death, they leave open the question whether some were created to meet then-current needs or to answer then-current questions. Also, Sunni and Shia collections contain reports that seem to confirm their separate beliefs and traditions. Historical puzzles like these are difficult, but the fact remains that for the vast majority of Muslims, the *hadith* are trusted as genuine, and authoritative, and as essential guides to understanding Muhammad, Islam, and the Qur'an.

The thousands of *hadith* cover a variety of topics, as readers will see when they browse through collections that are available online (e.g., https://sunnah.com). Here are some examples:

Narrated by Abdullah:
That the Messenger of Allah (🕌) said: "Whenever there are three of you, then let two not converse in exclusion of their companion." (al-Tirmidhi 2825)

Some *hadith* recall remarkable events, such as this one from Bukhari's collection:

Narrated by Sharik bin Abdullah bin Abi Namir: I heard Anas bin Malik saying, "On a Friday a person entered the main Mosque through the gate facing the pulpit while Allah's Messenger (🕌) was delivering the Khutba sermon. The man stood in front of Allah's Apostle and said, 'O Allah's Messenger (🕌)! The livestock are dying and the roads are cut off; so please pray to Allah for rain.'" Anas added, "Allah's Messenger (🕌) raised both his hands and said, 'O Allah! Bless us with rain! O Allah! Bless us with rain! O Allah! Bless us with rain!'" . . . Anas added, "A heavy cloud like a shield appeared from behind [Mount Sila]. When it came in the middle of the sky, it spread and then rained." Anas further said, "By Allah! We could not see the sun for a week." (Bukhari 1013)

This *hadith* goes on to say that it rained so long that the man had to ask Muhammad to reverse the process to end the rain. From this example, we can see the emphasis on the witness who observed the event and on those who transmitted the *hadith*. Many of the *hadith* deal with things that non-Muslims might consider mundane, but they illustrate the role of Muhammad's *sunna* in modeling all aspects of human experience.

Narrated by Abdullah bin Umar:
That the Prophet (🕌) said: "Let none of you eat with his left hand nor drink with his left hand, for indeed Satan eats with his left hand and drinks with his left hand." (al-Tirmidhi 1799)

Narrated by Al-Bara bin Azib:
"The Messenger of Allah (🕌) ordered us with seven things. . . . He ordered us to follow the funeral, visit the ill, reply to the sneezing person, accept the invitation, assist the oppressed, to help the one who made an oath, and to return the Salam greeting." (al-Tirmidhi 2809)

Muslims generally do not keep dogs as pets. This *hadith* explains why:

> Narrated by Abu Huraira:
> Allah's Messenger (ﷺ) said, "Whoever keeps a dog, one Qirat [a measurement] of the reward of his good deeds is deducted daily, unless the dog is used for guarding a farm or cattle." Abu Huraira (in another narration) said from the Prophet, "unless it is used for guarding sheep or farms, or for hunting." Narrated by Abu Hazim from Abu Huraira: "The Prophet (ﷺ) said, 'A dog is for guarding cattle or for hunting.'" (Bukhari 2322)

Muslims all over the world—especially now by way of the internet—have access to thousands of pieces of information reporting what Muhammad said and how he acted. Topics include almost every aspect of life—good manners, business, agriculture, how to brush one's teeth, behavior in marriage, prayer, dress and grooming, inheritance, food, and many more. These reports of the Prophet's *sunna* teach appropriate behavior for all Muslims. They are taught in schools, and much of the *sunna* has been put into Islamic law. Even informally through the examples of parents and others, the *hadith* show Muslims from childhood on what they should do and how they should act to be Muslims.

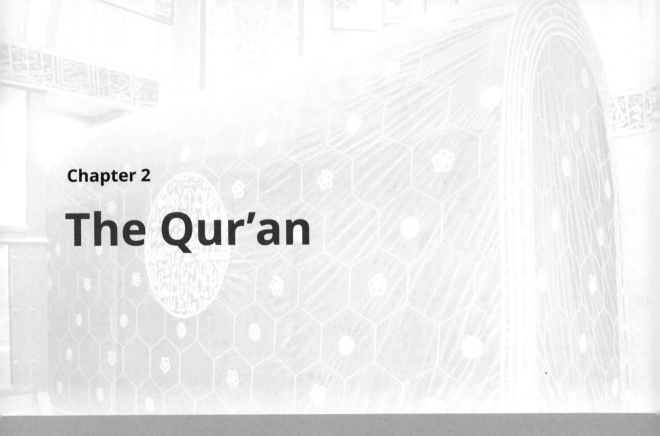

Chapter 2

The Qur'an

Terms and Names to Know

sura, Mutazilites, "occasions for revelation," *basmala*, *as-salamu alaykum*, *insha allah*, *al-hamdu li-llah*, calligraphy

The word *qur'an* means "recitation." The Qur'an (sometimes spelled Koran) is the recitation or pronouncement of Allah's word. About the size of the New Testament, it is very much *unlike* the New Testament in important ways. It is not a book of history. It does not tell a story, though there are several narratives in it. Instead, it is a collection of individual pronouncements in the words of Allah, each revealed separately at a specific point in history to meet the needs of the young Muslim community and the needs of the lasting Muslim community through all time. "We sent down unto thee the Book as a clarification of all things, and as a guidance and a mercy and glad tidings for those who submit" (16.89[N]). "We sent down the Qur'an with the truth, and with the truth it has come down" (17.105).

Content

The Qur'an contains 114 chapters, called *suras*, each an individual revelation. The *suras* vary in printed length from a few lines to thirty or so pages. Each *sura* has a name by which it is known; it is a word from the *sura* that sets it apart. The name does not necessarily represent the subject matter of the *sura*, but it usually is a term that is found near the beginning of it. For example, the fortieth through forty-sixth *suras* are named "The Forgiver," "Verses Made Clear," "Consultation," "Ornaments of Gold," "Smoke," "Kneeling," and "The Sand Dunes." To make navigation through the Qur'an more convenient, numbers have been assigned to the *suras* as well, and the *suras* are also divided into numbered verses.

The angel Gabriel was instrumental in revealing the *suras* to Muhammad. In the Qur'an, they are not in chronological order but are generally arranged from the longest to the shortest. They are not dated, and they contain no introductions that explain the historical settings in which they came. Muhammad, believed to be illiterate, was a conduit for the revelations and not the originator of any of the words or thoughts in them. Muslim tradition holds that when he uttered them, others memorized or wrote them down. The belief is that during the reign of the caliph Uthman, two decades after the Prophet's death, the entire body of *suras* was collected and arranged in the book as we have it today. Because the earliest extant manuscripts date to the ninth century, some historians believe that the Qur'an did not reach its final form until long after Muhammad's time.

Since early in Islamic history, both Muslim and non-Muslim scholars have endeavored to deduce from the content of the *suras* approximately when each was revealed in Muhammad's career, and some European-language translations have even printed the Qur'an in a proposed chronological order. Scholars divide the *suras* into two historical settings: the Meccan *suras* (those that came during the early Meccan period) and the Medinan *suras* (those that came while Muhammad and his followers lived in Medina). Traditional believers may find academic exercises of this sort to be irrelevant, but the division into the two periods is instructive, and it highlights distinctions between the two collections and the different life circumstances of the *umma* during the two periods.

The Meccan *suras* came when Islam was first being revealed. There was a Muslim community, but it was not a state, did not have a government, and thus did not have an emphasis on civil matters. The Meccan *suras* abound in doctrinal descriptions; they are the first revelations of the beliefs that would come to characterize the religion. In general, these *suras* are shorter than the later ones, and they contain general messages to believers and nonbelievers. They demonstrate how Islam was a new movement in the midst of unsympathetic and even hostile neighbors.

Most early copies of the Qur'an are preserved only in fragmentary form. This eighth-century copy is one of the oldest in existence. Missing only two pages, it is the oldest nearly complete Qur'an. Topkapı Palace Museum, Istanbul, Turkey.

When Muhammad moved the *umma* to Medina, the situation was different. He was now head of a government that required a new collection of civil, political, and legal regulations. The Medinan *suras*, as a consequence, presuppose the existence of an Islamic state. They are often long, regulatory, and legal and no longer give the impression that they come from a new religious movement but from an institutionalized civil society. They show greater awareness of and interaction with Jews and Christians, and they contain much more evidence of armed struggles against the Meccans and others.

Many readers recognize that the Qur'an's content reflects the Arabia of Muhammad's day, and he and the early Muslims are mentioned many times. The revelations, especially when read in a proposed chronological order, suggest a development or refinement of doctrines over time, and non-Muslim readers may see them as coming to Muhammad based on what was happening in the Muslim community or in response to questions Muhammad asked or in response to current events. But this is not how Muslims see them. They believe, instead, that the Qur'an has *always* existed.

In the ninth century, a group of rational thinkers called Mutazilites put forth philosophical arguments that the Qur'an did not always exist but is something that was created. Their reasoning was based on their belief in the total uniqueness of Allah (which we will discuss in chapter 4). If the Qur'an were eternal and uncreated, then there would be *two* eternal and uncreated realities—Allah and the Qur'an. The Mutazilites were not arguing that the Qur'an did not contain Allah's words, but if Allah uttered those words, how can they be as eternal as Allah himself?

Mainstream Muslims did not agree and rejected the idea that the Qur'an was created in Muhammad's day. If it were, Allah would be speaking in response to things that humans were doing, and he cannot be seen as dependent on human actions in any way. The revelations had to be eternal. Though the Qur'an always existed, Allah chose "occasions for revelation" to make its content known gradually to humankind. Those "occasions for revelation" are in harmony with what the book says about itself: "It is a recitation that We have revealed in parts, so that you can recite it to people at intervals; We have sent it down little by little" (17.106).

Muhammad does not speak in the Qur'an, nor does a narrator. Only Allah is the speaker. Usually he speaks in the royal voice of the first-person plural, "We," but on some occasions he refers to himself in the third person. In the *suras* he gives instructions both to Muhammad and to the community of believers, and he addresses unbelievers and sinners as well.

Subject Matter

The best way to characterize the subject matter of the Qur'an is to say that it consists of Islam's five main doctrines (Allah's oneness, angels, prophets, final judgment, and divine decree) and, to a lesser degree, Islam's five main worship practices (testifying, prayer, almsgiving, fasting, and pilgrimage). We will explore each of those topics in later chapters, but for now the point to be made is that the revelations deal with the basics of Islam. Readers find that there is a great deal of repetition in the *suras*, so much so that it has been stated without too much exaggeration that one can pick any fifteen consecutive verses in any *sura* and find each of the main doctrines in them. Readers also notice that in most of the *suras*, the subject matter moves freely from one topic to the next. The Qur'an may seem foreign to people who encounter it for the first time because of its use of unfamiliar phrases, but its overall message is clear. "It is [Allah] who has sent this Scripture

A sheet of the Qur'an dating to the eleventh century from Kairouan, Tunisia. The writing in black, red, and gold shows the great care exercised in creating the manuscript. Bardo Museum, Tunis, Tunisia.

down to you [Prophet]. Some of its verses are definite in meaning—these are the cornerstone of the Scripture—and others are ambiguous. . . . Those firmly grounded in knowledge say, 'We believe in it: it is all from our Lord'" (3.7).

In the Qur'an there is much appeal to earlier revelations, and several stories known from the Bible are repeated, though with details different from those in the Old and New Testaments. Twenty-four earlier prophets are mentioned by name: Adam, Idris (Enoch), Nuh (Noah), Ibrahim (Abraham), Lut (Lot), Ishaq (Isaac), Ismail (Ishmael), Yaqub (Jacob), Yusuf (Joseph), Musa (Moses), Harun (Aaron), Dawud (David), Sulayman (Solomon), Ilyas (Elijah), Alyasa (Elisha), Ayyub (Job), Yunus (Jonah), Dhu 'l-Kifl (perhaps Ezekiel), Zakariyya (Zachariah), Yahya (John the Baptist), Isa (Jesus), and the Arabian prophets Hud, Salih, and Shuayb. The presence of these names in the Qur'an is not incidental but emphasizes that the same Allah who revealed his will to those earlier prophets was now revealing his will to Muhammad. The stories are especially focused on the bad things that happened to earlier societies who rejected the words of the prophets. Thus one of the messages of the Qur'an, emphasized repeatedly, is its own legitimacy as Allah's word, as well as the legitimacy of the messenger Muhammad through whom Allah revealed it.

> You who believe, believe in God and His Messenger and in the Scripture He sent down to His Messenger, as well as what He sent down before. Anyone who does not believe in God, His angels, His Scriptures, His messengers, and the Last Day has gone far, far astray. . . . As He has already revealed to you [believers] in the Scripture, if you hear people denying and ridiculing God's revelation, do not sit with them unless they start to talk of other things, or else you yourselves will become like them: God will gather all the hypocrites and disbelievers together into Hell. (4.136, 140)

God's Word Made Book

If we are looking for analogies to help us understand what the Qur'an means to Muslims, we may be tempted to consider what the Bible means to Christians. But that analogy falls far short. More

A Qur'an reciter at a mosque in Belek, Turkey.

accurately, the Qur'an is to Muslims what Jesus Christ is to Christians. In Christianity Jesus is God incarnate—God's Word, character, attributes, and person revealed in human form. The Qur'an, for Muslims, serves the same role. It is God's Word, character, attributes, and person revealed in words in a book.

The Qur'an as a physical object and its words as words are as important as the book's message. Many Muslims have never read the Qur'an in its entirety, but they have heard and seen its phrases throughout their lives. Reciting its words is an act of worship, as is hearing it recited by others. Qur'an recitations are found twenty-four hours a day on radio stations in some Muslim lands, and one can easily watch and listen to recitations on internet video sites. Organizations sponsor competitions for reciters, and schools exist to teach the proper tones of recitation and to help young people memorize the entire book. Some Muslims have memorized whole *suras* without being able to understand what is in them. This may seem strange to Christians, for whom the meaning and content of the Bible are more important than the words, but for Muslims the divine words are holy even apart from what they mean. Reading or listening to the Qur'an is mostly a spiritual exercise, a sacrament, not a quest for information, but most Muslims aspire both to read and listen to the Qur'an and to understand its meaning for their lives.

How Muslims treat the Qur'an is another indicator of its importance. In Muslim homes, it is best to have it on the highest shelf and not beneath another book, and it is generally considered inappropriate to place it on the floor. When Muslims first enter a new house, they bring the Qur'an in as the first object to inhabit the home, providing a blessing for the home.

Because the Qur'an is eternal, is Allah's word, and is in the Arabic language, many Muslims will argue that it cannot be translated. No matter how faithful the translation, if it is changed into different words, it is no longer the Qur'an. Given Muslim sensitivities about the origin of the book, this is a persuasive argument, and thus some renderings into other languages have carefully worded titles: *The Qur'an: A Contemporary Understanding*; *The Meaning of the Holy Qur'an*; *English Translation of the Meaning of al-Qur'an*. Titles like these point out that what the reader has in her or his hands is not the Qur'an but an English translation of it.

The Qur'an's witness about itself is very clear: "God has sent down the most beautiful of all teachings: a Scripture that is consistent and draws comparisons; that causes the skins of those in awe of their Lord to quiver. Then their skins and their hearts soften at the mention of God: such is God's guidance. He guides with it whoever He will. . . . In this Qur'an, We have put forward all kinds of illustration for people, so that they may take heed—an Arabic Qur'an, free from any distortion—so that people may be mindful" (39.23, 27–28).

Interpreting the Qur'an

Muslim scholars began studying Islam very early. After the Prophet's death, the discipline of preserving the *hadith* reports began, and those remembrances can be called the original interpretation of the Qur'an because they preserve how Muhammad understood, applied, and lived it.

Muhammad ibn Jarir al-Tabari (838–923) was a scholar from Persia who wrote the earliest major commentary on the Qur'an that has survived. The *Tafsir al-Tabari* has been very influential since his time and is considered one of the best commentaries in existence. Much of its focus is on grammar and on the meaning of words, as al-Tabari parsed and analyzed the words and phrases in great detail to explore their meanings. One of the strengths of his commentary is that he included in it the interpretations of the earliest generations of Muslims—those who knew Muhammad and those who learned from people who knew Muhammad. His commentary is an enormous piece of scholarship, printed a century ago in thirty volumes and more recently in twelve volumes. It has never been translated in its entirety into English.

Ismail ibn Kathir (c. 1300–73) was another influential scholar who wrote a Qur'an commentary. A preacher at the Great Mosque in Damascus, he drew from al-Tabari but contributed much original material that has been highly valued historically. His commentary draws heavily from the *hadith* as a way to convey the meaning of the Qur'an as interpreted by the earliest Muslims.

These are early examples among many. Other scholars over the years have written commentaries or have used other means to analyze and interpret the text. These range from the grammatical and lexical interpretations of early scholars to the search for hidden meanings by mystics. That the Qur'an has yielded a variety of meanings has been seen by believers as a confirmation of its divine origin.

As can be imagined, each discussion of the Qur'an reflects the assumptions and perspectives of its author. Islam's two major divisions, the Sunnis and the Shia, have produced different interpretations based on their separate worldviews. But even within those divisions there are widely diverging strands of interpretation that are reflected in how Quranic texts are understood. Muslim scholars today still grapple with questions that have been around for centuries and others that are more recent. Because the Qur'an was revealed so long ago, much of the discussion has to do with how its words apply in our own day. Conservative traditionalists would argue that the specific commands in the text apply now as literally as they did in the seventh century. Most modernist interpreters, while believing just as fervently in the Qur'an as Allah's true revelation, argue instead that one must extract from the specifics the broader principles and moral messages and then apply those to the circumstances of our own time.

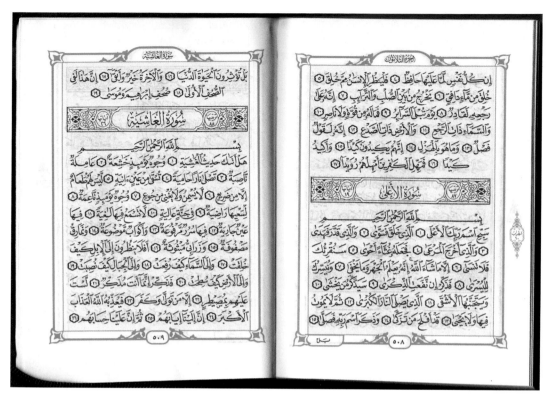

Suras 86–88 from a modern pocket-size, zipper-cover Qur'an.

Qur'anic Language in Speech and Art

Muslims from childhood are surrounded by Qur'anic language, even if they do not realize it. Phrases from the Qur'an are used in everyday speech in ways that remind them of Allah and of their obligations to him. We will look at four such phrases that every traveler in Muslim countries should be acquainted with.

bi-smi llahi ar-rahmani ar-rahim, "*In the name of Allah, the Compassionate, the Merciful.*" This phrase, called the *basmala*, begins each *sura* of the Qur'an except one (number 9). Muslims are encouraged to do all that they do in Allah's name, assuring the virtue of their activities and invoking Allah's blessings on them. Thus the phrase is used at the beginning of something written, before prayer, before eating, before public speaking, and before any other worthy pursuit. In calligraphy it adorns countless mosques, and it is found framed on the walls of countless offices, shops, and homes.

as-salamu alaykum, "Peace be upon you." This is an all-purpose Muslim greeting that wishes for the well-being of those one greets. Often one responds to it with *wa-alaykum as-salam*, "And upon you, peace."

insha allah, "If Allah wills." Islam teaches that humans, despite their grand pretensions, do not control the world nor their own destinies. It is in poor form to announce what will happen in a future that is not ours to predetermine. Thus one does not say words like "See you in the morning" without appending *insha allah* after those words (see 18.23–24). It may seem disconcerting to non-Muslims to hear the phrase after a commercial airline pilot announces a plane's itinerary, but it reminds Muslims that they and their lives are in Allah's hands.

al-hamdu li-llah, "Praise Allah." Devout Muslims know that if something good is happening in their lives, it is Allah's doing and not their own, and only Allah is deserving of the credit. Thus when one is asked about one's health with "How are you?" or something similar, the answer is *al-hamdu li-llah* because it acknowledges that one's well-being is a gift from Allah.

Executed in silver relief in beautiful calligraphy, this Qur'anic text is found in the al-Husayn Mosque in Cairo, Egypt.

In Islamic art, Allah is never to be depicted, and through much of Islamic history some purists have discouraged even the depiction of humans and other living things. There are exceptions, however, including in palaces and other secular spaces. In place of naturalistic images and with great respect for the words of Allah, early Muslims developed an art form out of the text. The oldest existing copies of the Qur'an show great effort to make the words on the pages as beautiful as possible, and those books are striking masterpieces.

Calligraphy is one of Islam's most characteristic esthetic endeavors. In almost any Islamic context, one can find Qur'anic words written in beautiful letters in a variety of amazing styles. Muslim artists and craftsmen have depicted the Qur'an's Arabic words very beautifully, often adapting the letters of the alphabet beyond readability. If many Arabs cannot read the Qur'anic calligraphy in their own native language, that is not to be lamented, because the words are sacred and manifest Allah's design even if they cannot be read. Mosques and shrines typically have Qur'anic passages on the walls and on domes that proclaim, with passages from the Qur'an, the greatness of Allah.

Chapter 3

After Muhammad

The death of Muhammad in 632 raised a number of hard questions for his followers. The majority view was that he made no arrangements for succession, and the Qur'an makes no mention of the subject. It was understood that there would be no further prophets and no more revelation after him, so the very idea of designating someone to succeed him was problematic. Would Muhammad's family have a role in leading the *umma* after his death? Would his tribe or his clan? How could any leaders after him obtain and retain legitimacy? One option that was not available was that the Muslims would simply go back to their homes and worship privately. The Qur'an does not envision that kind of world, and its later *suras* take for granted that Muslims would live in a community governed by Islam. The *umma* was to be not just a collection of believers but a political entity built and administered on Islamic principles. In addition, the Islamic state was already the government of most of Arabia by the time of the Prophet's death; there was already a "country" that needed to be governed, and Muhammad had set the precedent of adding new territory by alliance and conquest.

Caliphs

Muhammad's closest associates decided that to continue his work of leading the believers, a successor would need to be chosen, for which the Anglicized term is *caliph*. The caliphs were those who would lead in the coming generations.

The first caliph chosen was Abu Bakr, Muhammad's father-in-law and one of his first converts. He ruled for two years before dying of natural causes. He was succeeded by Umar, who was murdered after ten years in power. After him came Uthman, who ruled for twelve years before being murdered by dissidents. The fourth caliph was Ali, who was Muhammad's cousin and son-in-law, married to the Prophet's daughter Fatima. Ali was assassinated after five years. The untimely deaths of three of the first four caliphs is indicative of the fact that questions relating to succession and government were not easy ones, and not all early Muslims had the same perspective. The Sunnis, the majority division of Islam, identify these four caliphs as the "Rightly Guided Caliphs," believing that God blessed and guided their actions. They generally speak of them with respect. The division between the Sunnis and the Shia involved complicated politics and finally rested on the issue of succession. Shia Islam teaches that Muhammad's descendants through Ali and Fatima were designated by God to lead the Muslims, and thus God intended from the start that Ali would be the successor to Muhammad.

With Muhammad's death, the union of believers and Arabian tribes that he had put together was shaken, and several of the tribes which had sworn loyalty to him broke away. Abu Bakr had to act quickly and set about to reconquer Arabia. The reconquest was not completed until the time of Umar, who forgave the tribes that had broken away and brought them back to join in the continuing conquests. The apostasy and reconquest of the Arabians became a significant part of the early Muslim worldview and set two precedents that became increasingly important. First, one does not leave the *umma*. Once a nation or an individual becomes Muslim, it is never acceptable either to revert to previous status or to convert to something else. The second precedent was conquest. Where alliances and conversion were not possible, early Muslims sometimes used military conquest to increase the size of Muslim territory. Muhammad and Abu Bakr conquered Arabia, and Umar and Uthman continued the conquests on a scale that no one before Muhammad's time could have imagined.

Conquest

In the seventh century, there were two great imperial powers that had ruled the Near East for hundreds of years. In the west was the Byzantine (or Late Roman) Empire, and in the east was the Sasanian Persian Empire. The Persians were the heirs of the ancient Mesopotamian and Persian cultures with their rich heritage of science, learning, and art. Though many Christians lived within their realm, the state religion was Zoroastrianism, a faith that emphasized ethical behavior, the rejection of polytheism, and the worship of a true god who would provide a happy afterlife for the worthy. The Byzantines were the heirs of the culture and learning of the Greeks and Romans. They used the Aramaic language in Syria and Palestine but Latin or Greek in some other areas. The Byzantine religion was Orthodox Christianity, with its emphasis on doctrine and on church administration by priests, bishops, and patriarchs.

By the time of Muhammad's death, the Romans and the Persians had been fighting each other intermittently for over five hundred years, contending over the territories between them. Because of war, plague, and societal decay, both empires were exhausted economically, and both were having difficulties keeping their vast territories under control. There was much discontent in

Selected Dates in Islamic History

Muhammad's death 632
Abu Bakr 632–34
Umar 634–44
Conquest of Jerusalem 638
Uthman 644–56
Ali 656–61
Battle of the Camel 656
Umayyad Empire 661–750

Battle of Karbala 680
Dome of the Rock built 691
Abbasid Empire 750–1258
Crusades 1095–1302
Ayyubid Empire 1174–1260
Mamluk Empire 1250–1517
Ottoman Empire c. 1300–1923
Safavid Empire (Persia) 1501–1736
Mughal Empire (India) 1526–1857

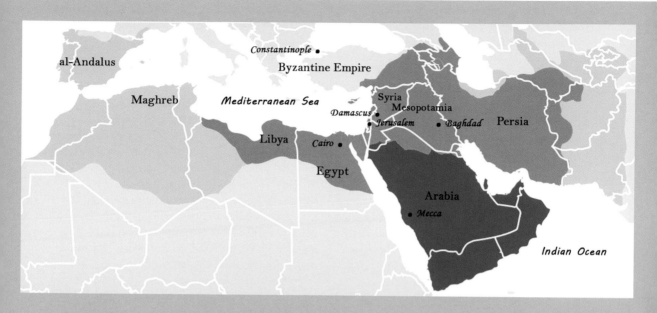

At the time of Muhammad, the Byzantine Empire controlled much of the area on this map immediately to the west of Mesopotamia, both north and south of the Mediterranean Sea. The Persians controlled Mesopotamia and the area to the east. The dark rust color represents Muslim-controlled territory at the time of Muhammad's death (632), orange represents lands conquered during the reigns of the Rightly Guided Caliphs (632–61), and yellow represents lands conquered during the reign of the Umayyads (661–750).

Byzantine lands, often centered around doctrinal issues that divided the Orthodox emperors from many of their subject peoples. Christianity was highly fragmented. The Persian Empire, for its part, was in a state of terminal decline and was just a shell of what it had been in earlier times. Into this situation came the armies out of Arabia, led or sent by Umar and later by Uthman, moving into territories that the two great powers could no longer defend. In a few short years, the Arab armies conquered over half of the Byzantine realm and all of the Persian Empire.

It may seem odd to modern readers that an army associated with a religious movement would be motivated by conquest and plunder, but in this the Muslim armies were no different from other ancient conquerors. The creation of an extensive empire enriched the conquerors, allowed Islam to be spread far beyond the borders of Arabia, and confirmed in the minds of the believers that God was blessing their cause with success. Unlike many earlier conquerors, the Muslim Arabs usually did not destroy existing cities but allowed them to

continue to thrive, which many of them did under new imperial administration. Following military conquest, the new rulers established Arab garrison settlements in the newly occupied territories, often adjacent to established population centers. Populated by governors, soldiers, and in some areas by settlers from Arabia, those communities grew in size and influence into what eventually became mixed-culture urban areas.

Arabization and Islamization

Two gradual processes—Arabization and Islamization—followed in the conquered territories, both lasting centuries to make the Middle East what it is today. Initially the new rulers kept the existing civil structures in power and retained the languages of local administrations—Latin, Greek, Aramaic, and Persian. But as the Arabs became more entrenched and prosperous in their new lands, the Arabic language gradually replaced native languages—Aramaic in Mesopotamia, Syria, and Palestine; and Greek and Latin in

North Africa. Over the course of generations, the language of the new rulers became the language of most of the population. Thus the people there became *Arabs* as they are today—native speakers of Arabic. East of Mesopotamia, in contrast, the Persian language has prevailed to the present.

The Arabs made good use of the culture and technology of the lands they conquered. Engineering and architecture in the early centuries came from the Romans and the Persians. The earliest Islamic buildings, for example, consist of Byzantine architectural styles decorated with Islamicized-Byzantine or Islamicized-Persian art. In due time, however, the Muslims developed distinctive art forms of their own that expressed Islamic culture and religion in unique and creative ways.

The Islamization of the Near East was also a slow process, and it was never completed in some regions. As the Qur'an envisions Muslims living in a state established on and guided by the principles of Islam, the new empire was always intended to be an Islamic realm with Islamic rulers and laws. Islam provided a separate status for the conquered peoples. A non-Muslim was called a *dhimmi* and was governed by different laws than those that applied to Muslims, with certain protections but also with significant restrictions. Among other things, *dhimmi*s were required to pay a special tax. Though conversion was not imposed on them, the distinct advantages of full citizenship and full engagement in society were among the reasons why untold thousands over the course of time embraced Islam. Jews and Christians, while not enjoying all the benefits of Islamic citizenship, were acknowledged as "People of the Book," with special protections because they were governed by holy books. Later, Zoroastrians were added to the list, and later still, Hindus and Buddhists in India. Although the *dhimmi* system no longer exists today as it did at the time of the early Islamic empire, some Muslim-majority countries continue to place legal restrictions on non-Muslim communities within their lands.

Ali, Umayyads, and Abbasids

After Ali became the caliph, he moved the capital into what is now Iraq. Arabia would never again be the political center of gravity of a Muslim empire, but because the holy cities Mecca and Medina were there, it would remain the destination of pilgrimages for Muslims from around the world.

Ali's tenure as caliph was not an easy one. He had the support of those who believed Muhammad's descendants should rule, but other Arabian tribal groups felt entitled as well. In the year 656, an army of Muslims from Medina led by Muhammad's wife Aisha attacked Ali and his followers. It was the Battle of the Camel—so named because Aisha herself mounted a camel and participated in the conflict. Ali was later murdered by a member of an extremist Islamic group called the Kharijites. The Kharijites had broken with the main body of Muslims because they felt that the *umma* had become corrupt, and they wanted to purify it. They believed that anyone they considered a sinner was no longer a Muslim but an apostate who would go to hell, and some of their members believed that people like that should be killed. They believed they had the right to strike against others to enforce their strict views and even to attack rulers. This was an early doctrinal challenge within Islam. The mainstream rejected the Kharijites' ideas, but as we will see later in this book, the instincts that motivated the Kharijites did not die with them.

Ali's son Hasan, Muhammad's grandson, ruled as the next caliph for only a short time before abdicating to the superior forces of Muawiya, the governor of Damascus. Muawiya was from the Umayyad clan, which had aspirations to rule. The followers and family of Ali still made claims to the caliphate in the person of Ali's second son, Husayn. In the Battle of Karbala in 680, Umayyad forces massacred Husayn and his supporters.

The Umayyad dynasty that Muawiya established lasted less than a century (661–750), but it was a time of massive expansion of the Islamic realm. Under Umar and Uthman, Islam had spread from Persia in the east to Algeria in the west. Under the Umayyads, the empire extended to the borders of India in the east, all the way to the Atlantic Ocean in the west, and from there north into southern France. During the Umayyad caliphate with its capital in Damascus, Palestine and Syria flourished. Jerusalem became a major city, and in it the Umayyads built the two great mosques that still stand today—the Dome of the Rock and the al-Aqsa (now much changed and

The Dome of the Rock, built by the Umayyad caliph Abd al-Malik in 691, was intended to send a clear signal of Islam's supremacy not only over Jerusalem but also over the two previous Abrahamic religions—Judaism and Christianity.

rebuilt). Monumental Umayyad mosques were also built in Damascus and Aleppo, and desert castles provided winter retreats for the rulers.

Jerusalem's Dome of the Rock, built in 691, is Islam's oldest existing building. Its design and inscriptions shows that it was never intended as a congregational mosque but as a monument with more symbolic purposes. It was built on the site of Jerusalem's two earlier Israelite temples, showing Islam as the legitimate successor to that holy space and to the previous revelations. Abraham's traditional association with the site was not lost on the builders, and the shrine would forever announce the Muslim claim that he, the father of the Arabs as well as the Jews, was a believer in the one true faith that the Muslim conquerors had restored to Jerusalem. The architecture is Byzantine, with an octagonal design normally reserved for the holiest of Christian churches. Words inscribed on the

walls inside are of particular importance. In the absence of earlier manuscripts, they are probably the oldest preserved passages of the Qur'an. The texts selected are messages to Christians that their beliefs are wrong, that Jesus is not God's son, and that Islam is God's true religion. With its mosaics showing jewels and crowns, the shrine likewise uses signs of the royal power of the conquered empires. In short, the Dome of the Rock, on its high platform visible from every direction, was an announcement of Islamic supremacy.

In 750 the Umayyads were conquered by a rival group from Mesopotamia and Persia, the Abbasids, who were descendants of Muhammad's uncle. The time of the Abbasid caliphate (750–1258) was an era of tremendous cultural and intellectual attainment. Needing a new capital city from which to rule the vast Islamic domain, the second Abbasid caliph founded the city of

Baghdad in 762, causing Damascus and Jerusalem to become increasingly less important. Baghdad would stand for half a millennium as a great Islamic center until it was destroyed in 1258 by Mongol invaders. The empire, however, did not stay intact during all of those years, and it underwent numerous divisions as local rulers in distant locations slowly usurped regional power from the caliphs in Baghdad. As a consequence, other important centers of Islamic culture were established as well. The area of Cairo, Egypt, was conquered by Muslim invaders during the caliphate of Umar, less than ten years after Muhammad's death. An early Islamic settlement there grew to become one of the great cities of the world. From Baghdad, Cairo, and other cities, a robust Islamic artistic and intellectual tradition followed.

Later Developments

Jerusalem had been a Christian city from the early fourth century until the caliph Umar conquered it in 638. In the coming centuries, many of the Christians living in Palestine gradually became Arabized and Islamized. Medieval Christians in Western Europe believed it was their obligation to liberate the Holy Land from the Muslims, so beginning near the end of the eleventh century they launched a series of invasions into the Middle East with that in mind. Those invasions, the Crusades, lasted for over two centuries (1095–1302), with not much to show for them but death, destruction, and castles that still stand today. The Muslim commander Saladin, who defeated the Crusaders and reestablished Jerusalem as a Muslim city, remains an important Middle Eastern hero.

Saladin and his descendants, the Ayyubid dynasty, ruled over much of the Middle East for about a century (1174–1260), and they in turn were replaced by the Mamluk Empire that lasted over two hundred years (1250–1517). Both of those empires endured ongoing civil wars, making the Middle East a frequent scene of conflict. The Mamluks left their imprint in lasting ways, however, with mosques, palaces, and tombs that can still be seen today in cities like Cairo, Jerusalem, and Damascus.

The dynasty that would stay in power the longest in the Middle East and would last into the modern period would be the Ottoman Turks (c. 1300–1923). With their capture of Constantinople (now Istanbul) in 1453, they brought to an end the Byzantine Empire and finally established Islam's supremacy over all of the Middle East. Now Istanbul became Islam's greatest center. In 1517 the Ottomans conquered Mecca, Medina, and Jerusalem from the Mamluks, thus bringing all three of Islam's holiest cities into their hands. Roughly contemporary with the Ottomans were the Safavids in Persia (1501–1736) and the Mughals in India (1526–1857). The Safavid shahs made Shiism the state religion in Persia, which has had important implications in Iran since that time. The Mughals were a Muslim dynasty that ruled over a Hindu-majority population. All three of those vast empires were weakened in later centuries by European colonialism and advances in European technology and economy.

Early Islam and the West

Europeans sometimes take credit for inventing universities and higher education, but the Muslim claim is stronger. Early in Islamic history, advanced schools called *madrasas* were established. They were broad-ranging schools that taught a variety of disciplines. One of them, Qarawiyyin University in Morocco, dates to 859 and is now often considered the oldest continually operating university in the world. By the ninth century there were medical schools in Muslim lands. Al-Azhar University in Cairo, established in 975 and still open today, taught law, grammar, astronomy, philosophy, logic, and other secular topics, as well as Islamic studies. Schools like these became the models for universities in Bologna in 1088, Paris in 1150, and Oxford in 1167.

The Crusades and the long-lasting Muslim presence in Spain gave much of Western Europe its first exposure to Islamic civilization. Through that exposure, Westerners became aware of the sciences that Muslim scholars were researching and writing about. Advances in astronomy, mathematics, and natural science placed the Islamic world generations ahead of the West, and some Arabic vocabulary in those fields made its way into European languages, such as *alcohol*, *algebra*, *lemon*, *spinach*, and *zenith*. Western Europe in the tenth to thirteenth centuries was composed of what we now call "developing nations,"

Istanbul's Sultanahmet Mosque, also called the Blue Mosque, is a high point of Ottoman artistic expression. Constructed in the early seventeenth century, it expands, like many other Ottoman mosques, on the Byzantine design of the Hagia Sophia, Constantinople's great imperial Christian church. This is seen in its domes and semi-domes that create an enormous prayer hall under a spreading central dome. Sultanahmet has six minarets.

while Islam had become heir to much of the intellectual heritage of Egypt, Greece, Rome, Mesopotamia, and Persia. It was Muslims who preserved many of the great Classical Greek and Latin texts, which would otherwise now be lost. Muslims likewise preserved and transmitted much of Greek and Roman philosophy. In the decades after the Crusades, Western Europe's contact with the Islamic world would plant some of the seeds for what we now call the Renaissance—the "rebirth" of classical culture, and thus the birth of modern Western civilization.

Chapter 4

Five Basic Beliefs

Islam is identified by its five basic beliefs and five basic worship practices. Those are lists that were developed early in Islamic history and serve as a useful way to describe the religion. In later chapters we will look at the basic worship practices, and in this chapter we will examine the fundamental beliefs. A *hadith* quotes Muhammad saying that Islam is "to believe in Allah, His angels, His Books, His Messengers, and the Last Day, and that you believe in preordainment (destiny), its bad and good consequences" (Riyad as-Salihin 60). The five main beliefs are (1) God's oneness, (2) angels, (3) prophets and scripture, (4) final judgment, and (5) divine decree and predestination.

At the outset, it is important to note that because Islam has no central authority, there is no single voice to interpret its teachings. Thus the beliefs in this chapter have been interpreted in different ways since the beginning of Islam. Some of the interpretations that are widely accepted today were debated vigorously in the earliest centuries and came about only as the result of

historical conflicts between majority Muslims and dissidents who asked hard questions. We will rely on passages from the Qur'an to help us understand these beliefs as many Muslims understand them today.

The Oneness of God—*tawhid*

Islam is strictly monotheistic, recognizing the existence of only one god. The Arabic word *Allah* means "God"—more accurately, "the God"—and it also serves as God's name. Muslims, Jews, and Christians all believe in the same deity, though the three religions understand God differently.

The word *tawhid* is translated as "oneness," yet it implies more than the idea that Allah is the only divine being. The word suggests his unity, his uniqueness, his wholeness, and his self-sufficiency.

In Muhammad's world, the idea of Allah's oneness stood in sharp contrast to the religions of his pagan contemporaries, who believed in many deities and worshipped them at the Kaaba.

The Qur'an states, "He, God, is One, God, the Eternally Sufficient unto Himself. He begets not; nor was He begotten. And none is like unto Him" (112^N). The Muslim concept stands in sharp contrast to the beliefs of Christianity, because Jesus, according to the New Testament, is divine, "equal with God" (Philippians 2:6), and God's son (Matthew 16:16). The Orthodox Christians whom early Muslims encountered argued that God, Jesus, and the Holy Spirit were members of the Trinity of three persons, a concept that Muslims believed bordered on polytheism and clearly violated the doctrine of God's oneness.

In Islam there is no need for Jesus's suffering and death to atone for human sinfulness. Allah can forgive whom he will, and thus no intercessor is needed between him and humankind. Jesus, though an important prophet, is not a savior, is not divine, is not God's son, and was not crucified. "The disbelievers say, 'The Lord of Mercy has offspring.' How terrible is this thing you assert: it almost causes the heavens to be torn apart, the earth to split asunder, the mountains to crumble to pieces, that they attribute offspring to the Lord of Mercy" (19.88–91). The Qur'anic inscriptions inside the Dome of the Rock that we encountered in chapter 3 were carefully selected to announce that Jesus was only a prophet and not divine.

Allah is not merely the only god there is, but he is in every way unique, complete, and in need of nothing. He is not like his creations in any way, and nothing in all of existence can be like him. The most unforgivable of all sins is *shirk*, the association of anything with Allah, whether it be through polytheism, through making images of him, or through other means. The idea that humans are God's children is not acceptable, nor that humans can in any way be like him, nor that he can have a shape or be in a place or in a time.

Readers sometimes notice that the Qur'an contains some anthropomorphic references to Allah, where he is depicted in human-like ways as seeing, hearing, sitting on a throne, and so forth. How should readers reconcile those passages with the idea that Allah is not at all like humans? The Mutazilites from the ninth century that we met in chapter 2 typically applied reason and logic to questions like this. They argued that the anthropomorphisms applied to Allah were all simply metaphors. Some accepted that view, yet the idea of asserting that one can reject a literal reading of the Qur'an made many people uncomfortable. Later theologians acknowledged that this was a difficult conundrum. They ruled that although one must not state that those words in the Qur'an are metaphors, Allah is nonetheless unlike those of us who see, hear, have eyes, and sit. How the two ideas could be reconciled would remain unexplained.

Angels

Allah and humans are not the only intelligent beings who inhabit the universe. Angels exist in large numbers and serve Allah as he wills. Their

Most mosques display the name *Allah* prominently, and many Sunni mosques display a series of plaques or medallions with the names of Allah, Muhammad, and the Rightly Guided Caliphs. The calligraphic medallions in the Hagia Sophia in Istanbul—including this one of Allah and the matching ones with the names of the caliphs—are the largest ones in the world, measuring 7.5 meters in diameter. Allah is written in large letters, and on the left in smaller letters is "May he be exalted," a phrase often uttered after a mention of Allah.

The angel Israfil, who will blow his trumpet to announce the day of resurrection. In Islam there are thousands of angels who perform a variety of functions in God's service. A few have special status, including Israfil; Mikail (Michael), who helps oversee the forces of nature; and Jibril (Gabriel), who revealed the Qur'an to Muhammad. From a thirteenth-century manuscript; Freer Gallery of Art, Washington, DC.

functions are varied, but all that they do is in Allah's service to further his work. They praise him night and day (21.19–20). They act as his messengers, such as Jibril (Gabriel), who brought the first revelation of the Qur'an to Muhammad. Allah "made angels messengers with two, three, four [pairs of] wings" (35.1). They serve as guards of hell and as attendants in paradise. They watch over people and record their deeds. They assisted the early Muslims to victory in their battles.

Angels are made of light, and Allah created them before he created humans. Because they are unseen and of the heavenly realm, they cannot be comprehended fully by mortals. The Qur'an seems to say that they are not females, but because it does not call them males, some Muslims believe that they are neither. Allah causes them to appear in human form if necessary, but they are not humans, and humans in the hereafter will not become as they are. Angels are sinless and always obedient, and they have no agency because they exist solely to do Allah's will.

Jinn are a different category of beings, made of fire. The word *jinn* is a collective term, and the singular form, *jinni*, has made its way into English as "genie." These beings are often associated with the mysterious and unseen forces that plague humans with misfortune and make life unpredictable and dangerous, though some *jinn* are good. The Qur'an reveals that they are created beings, made by Allah to worship him: "I created the jinn and mankind only that they might worship Me" (51.56). They usually live on this earth in dark, unclean places. Like humans, they have agency to obey or disobey Allah, and their agency is what leads to their sometimes malevolent behavior. A *hadith* suggests that all humans are accompanied by *jinn*. Aisha, the Prophet's wife, reported this conversation. She asked, "Allah's Messenger, is there along with me a devil [i.e., *jinni*]? He said: Yes. I said: Is a devil attached to everyone? He said: Yes. I (Aisha) again said: Allah's Messenger, is it with you also? He said: Yes, but my Lord [Allah] has helped me against him and as such I am absolutely safe from his mischief" (Muslim 2815). Another version of this tradition reports that the *jinni* associated with the Prophet motivates him only to do good (Muslim 2814a). Indeed, some *jinn*, like some humans, have heard the Qur'an and have become believers. A *sura* quotes their words: "We have heard a wondrous Qur'an, that gives guidance to righteousness, and we have come to believe it. . . . Some of us submit to Him and others go the wrong way: those who submit to God have found wise guidance, but those who go wrong will be fuel for Hellfire" (72.1–2, 14–15).

The most destructive of the *jinn* is Iblis, also called Satan. His fall came at the time when Allah created the first man:

> We also created man out of dried clay formed from dark mud—the jinn We created before, from the fire of scorching wind. Your Lord said to the angels, "I will create a mortal out of dried clay, formed from dark mud. When I have

fashioned him and breathed My spirit into him, bow down before him," and the angels all did so. But not Iblis: he refused to bow down like the others.

God said, "Iblis, why did you not bow down like the others?" and he answered, "I will not bow to a mortal You created from dried clay, formed from dark mud." "Get out of here!" said God. "You are an outcast, rejected until the Day of Judgement." Iblis said, "My Lord, give me respite until the Day when they are raised from the dead." "You have respite," said God, "until the Day of the Appointed Time." Iblis then said to God, "Because You have put me in the wrong, I will lure mankind on earth and put them in the wrong, all except Your devoted servants." God said, "[Devotion] is a straight path to Me: you will have no power over My servants, only over the ones who go astray and follow you. Hell is the promised place for all these." (15.26–43; cf. 18.50)

Prophets and Scripture

As we have seen, the Qur'an teaches of a long line of prophets that culminated in the life of Muhammad, who would be the last and greatest of them all. Prophets are generally considered to be sinless, but they are mortal men with a divine mission. Their calling, as Allah told Muhammad, is "Remind them: your only task is to remind, you are not there to control them" (88.21).

Some of the prophets are familiar from the Bible. Abraham "was a man of truth, a prophet. He said to his father, 'Father, why do you worship something that can neither hear nor see nor benefit you in any way?' . . . We granted him Isaac and Jacob and made them both prophets: We granted Our grace to all of them, and gave them a noble reputation. . . . Mention too, in the Scripture, the story of Ishmael. He was true to his promise, a messenger and a prophet. . . . [Enoch] was a man of truth, a prophet. We raised him to a high position" (19.41–42, 49–50, 54, 56–57).

Despite the fact that Allah provided prophets for the various nations, in every case the people rebelled against him, abandoned true religion, and entered into periods of confusion and apostasy.

Some prophets have an additional title, *rasul*, which is often translated as "apostle" or "messenger." The Qur'an does not describe the difference between a prophet and a *rasul*, but it appears that a *rasul* is one who has a special calling to a specific nation, sometimes accompanied by the revelation of a book. Among those identified as *rasuls* in the Qur'an are Moses, Jesus, and Muhammad. "We gave Moses the Scripture to provide insight, guidance, and mercy for people, so that they might take heed" (28.43). Jesus said, "I am a servant of God. He has granted me the Scripture; made me a prophet" (19.30). History repeated itself even

Four of the prophets Muhammad encountered on his Night Journey and Ascension. He spoke on that journey with several prophets, including Adam, John the Baptist, Jesus, Joseph, Idris (Enoch), Aaron, Moses, and Abraham. They, like Muhammad, are depicted with flaming nimbuses (halos) around their heads, showing their holiness and emphasizing the special role and status prophets have in Islam. From a fifteenth-century manuscript, Afghanistan; Bibliothèque nationale de France.

after Moses and Jesus revealed holy books to their people, so in the end Allah called Muhammad: "These are the verses of the Scripture that makes things clear—We have sent it down as an Arabic Qur'an so that you [people] may understand" (12.1–2). "This revelation is no fabrication: it is a confirmation of the truth of what was sent before it; an explanation of everything; a guide and a blessing for those who believe" (12.111). "Let there be no doubt about it, it is from the Lord of all worlds" (10.37).

The Qur'an is thus not the first scripture Allah made known, but it will be the last. It is evidence of Allah's continuing work among many nations to give them his true religion. That true religion, in every time period, was Islam. "He has laid down for you [people] the same commandment that He gave Noah, which We have revealed to you [Muhammad] and which We enjoined on Abraham and Moses and Jesus" (42.13). As the final revelation, the Qur'an was not only to place Allah's truth back on the earth for the last time but also to confirm all of the previous truths as well.

Final Judgment

The religions of the Ancient Near East placed very little emphasis on an afterlife. For most people, the purpose of religion was to please the gods in order to obtain their favor for earthly matters—fertility of crops, flocks, and herds. Christianity was an exception, with teachings of a physical resurrection and a glorious afterlife for those who in this life follow Jesus.

The Qur'an is clear on the topic of life after death: God "causes [each human] to die and be buried. When He wills, He will raise him up again" (80.21–22). Islam not only assures all of a resurrection, but it also assures that people will be judged based on their actions in life and will be assigned either to paradise or to hell. "On that Day, man will be told what he put first and what he put last. Truly, man is a clear witness against himself, despite all the excuses he may put forward" (75.13–15). "Those who did well will have the best reward and more besides. . . . As for those who did evil, each evil deed will be requited by its equal and humiliation will cover them" (10.26–27).

The Qur'an presents a tangible afterlife that will include the kinds of pleasures and pains that humans experience now but to a much greater degree. The afterlife as described in the Qur'an is neither mystical, spiritual, nor ethereal but is something all readers can understand based on their own human experience. Yet, as with many other Qur'anic ideas, interpretations range from the very literal to the very metaphorical.

The Arabic word usually translated as "hell" means "the fire." It is a punitive existence rather than a redemptive one, and it will be the just reward for those who will dwell there. Those who are consigned to it will experience "chains, iron collars, and blazing Fire" (76.4). "When their skins have been burned away, We shall replace them with new ones so that they may continue to feel the pain" (4.56). "Some faces on that Day will be downcast, toiling and weary, as they enter the blazing Fire and are forced to drink from a boiling spring, with no food for them except bitter dry thorns that neither nourish nor satisfy hunger" (88.2–7). There "they will taste no coolness nor drink except one that is scalding" (78.24–25), "a scalding, dark, foul fluid" (38.57). People in paradise will ask those in hell, "'What drove you to the Scorching Fire?' and they will answer, 'We did not pray; we did not feed the poor; we indulged with others [in mocking the believers]; we denied the Day of Judgement until the Certain End came upon us'" (74.42–47).

Paradise will be very different. It will be the reward for "the believers," or, frequently, those who "believe and do good deeds" (29.9). It will be a luxuriant well-watered garden abounding in trees and shade. For dwellers in the dry climate of Arabia, with few forests and scarce water sources, it will be an eternity of the most pleasant things they could imagine. "Those who believe and do good deeds. . . . Their reward with their Lord is everlasting Gardens graced with flowing streams, where they will stay forever" (98.7–8). They will be "with their righteous ancestors, spouses, and descendants" (13.23). "They will sit on couches, feeling neither scorching heat nor biting cold, with shady [branches] spread above them and clusters of fruit hanging close at hand. . . . If you looked around you would see bliss and great opulence: they will wear garments of green silk and brocade; they will be adorned with silver bracelets;

their Lord will give them a pure drink" (76.13–14, 20–21). "You will recognize on their faces the radiance of bliss" (83.24).

Muslim commentators since the beginning have discussed the nature of good and evil and what level of wickedness one must exercise in order to be worthy of the fires of hell. The Qur'an repeatedly states that "unbelievers," those who disbelieve Islam and the Qur'an, will spend their eternity suffering. "Those who disbelieve and deny Our signs, it is they who are the inhabitants of the Fire, abiding therein" (2.39[N]). "Whosoever seeks a religion other than submission [Islam], it shall not be accepted of him, and in the Hereafter he shall be among the losers" (3.85[N]). Many Muslims today are firmly committed to this absolutist position, and some sources argue that the good deeds of unbelievers can only be rewarded in this life but not in the next. I was once told by the imam of a mosque that because I have read the Qur'an and

Paradise, as shown to Muhammad on his Night Journey and Ascension. Notice that paradise includes fond associations with others and also the presence of beautiful trees, flowers, and birds. From a fifteenth-century manuscript, Afghanistan; Bibliothèque nationale de France.

yet did not convert to Islam, I will spend eternity in hell. Other Islamic scholars have told me that if I am a good Christian, I will be with them in paradise, reflecting a position that many Muslims hold. Some commentators since the beginning have even discussed whether, or for whom, hell will be a permanent condition or a temporary punishment. The answer most Muslims give to questions like these is perhaps the best: "Only God knows."

In either case, the Qur'an points out with considerable emphasis that Allah's decisions about our ultimate future will be just. All "will be judged with justice and will not be wronged" (10.54). Thus, whether one goes to paradise or into the fire, it will be because one deserves it.

Divine Decree and Predestination

For some Muslims, this topic is straightforward and easy to comprehend: Allah determines all of our actions in advance. Every good thing we do, and even every wicked thing we do is Allah's doing. He makes them happen. Moreover, Allah also predestines—determines in advance—whether we will go to paradise or to hell.

The fundamental understanding of Allah's divine will and determination is that he has decreed all things, and all things happen because he wills them to happen. But even though this is one of the main doctrines of Islam, exactly what it means has been a matter of debate since shortly after the time of Muhammad. Those who advocated a free-will position, like the Mutazilites, argued that only with truly free will could people be responsible for their actions and their fate. If there were no free will, then Allah could not be just in his rewards and punishments.

The evidence in the Qur'an is mixed, and there are passages that can be set forward that support a free-will position as well as a position of predestination. The *hadith* emphasize Allah's predetermination. One *hadith* reports Muhammad's teaching that when a child is in his mother's womb, Allah sends an angel with instructions to write four things about the child: his livelihood, the date of his death, his deeds, and whether he will go to hell or to paradise (Bukhari 7454).

Admittedly, this question was more important among philosophers and theologians in Islamic history than it is in the lives of ordinary Muslims today. As I have asked Muslims whether they have free will, invariably they believe they do and find the question puzzling.

God's sovereignty seems to be the issue. If humans have true agency, then there is something in the universe that God cannot control. This has been an uncomfortable idea for Muslim theologians over the centuries, as it has for Christian theologians as well. Genuine human agency suggests that there are limits to God's power. A solution proposed in the early centuries of Islam is that Allah does determine in advance the things we do, but in the process of actually doing those things, we *acquire* them and own them ourselves, thereby becoming accountable for them. Thus, in Allah's justice, sinners will receive the fate that they deserve, and "no soul shall suffer the least injustice. You shall be rewarded according only to your deeds" (36.54). Not surprisingly, there are Muslim thinkers today who are not comfortable with this solution, so the quest to better understand the meaning of the doctrine continues.

Chapter 5

Witness, Prayer, and Almsgiving

Terms and Names to Know

shahada, salat, qibla, allahu akbar, imam, *zakat*

Several *hadith* provide the title for the basic worship practices that all Muslims are to observe: "It is narrated on the authority of Abdullah son of Umar that the Messenger of Allah (ﷺ) said: (The superstructure of) al-Islam is raised on five (pillars), testifying (the fact) that there is no god but Allah, that Muhammad is His bondsman and messenger, and the establishment of prayer, payment of zakat, pilgrimage to the House (Kaaba), and the fast of Ramadan" (Muslim 16c). These observances are the "Five Pillars of Islam." We will discuss three of them in this chapter: witness, prayer, and almsgiving. In the following chapter we will look at fasting during the month of Ramadan and the pilgrimage to Mecca.

In some religions (such as Catholic and Orthodox Christianity), there are priests who perform rituals in behalf of worshippers that worshippers are not empowered to perform themselves. Islam is a very egalitarian religion, and it is remarkable that its major worship practices, including those described below and in chapter 6,

are actions that can be performed by any Muslim without a need for intervention by anyone else.

Witness of Faith (*shahada*)

The Sunni *shahada* is a very simple statement of faith: *la ilaha illa-llah, muhammadun rasulu-llah,* "There is no god but Allah. Muhammad is the messenger of Allah." The Shia *shahada* is somewhat different and will be seen in chapter 9.

The word *shahada* means "witness," from a verb that means "testify" or "witness." Many

The *shahada* in calligraphy.

religions have creedal statements that identify their fundamental beliefs. Most are long and attempt to be somewhat comprehensive, including the Nicene and Apostles' Creeds that are accepted by most Christians, and some are much more detailed than those. The *shahada* may be unique in its brevity, but Muslims believe it to be comprehensive and sufficient. All of Islam is contained in it: Allah is the only god, and all of the revelations, actions, and teachings of his messenger Muhammad are authoritative.

But the *shahada* is more than a list of what Muslims believe. It is a statement of witness from the one who utters it. When babies are first born, the *shahada* is whispered into their ears and from that moment on they are Muslims. When one wants to convert to Islam, there is no equivalent to baptism as in the Christian tradition. The only ritual is simply to pronounce the words of the *shahada*, but one must say them with full intent and understand them the way Muslims do. One does this in Arabic and in front of witnesses.

Believing and uttering the *shahada* makes a person a Muslim and places her or him on the path to Islamic living, a path that includes continuing obligations to Allah. Among those are the pillars that follow.

Prayer (*salat*)

The *salat* is one of the most widely recognized features of Islam. It is prayer, but it is prayer unlike what many non-Muslims have experienced. It is a sequence of ritual motions that worshippers undertake (standing, bowing, and kneeling) during which they utter words that accompany those motions. During Muhammad's Night Journey and Ascension, he received from Allah the command for Muslims to pray five times daily. Today devout Muslims pray in the early morning, at noon, at midafternoon, at sunset, and in the evening. "Keep up regular prayer, for prayer is obligatory for the believers at prescribed times" (4.103). Because the times of sunrise and sunset change with each passing day, the prayer times change daily as well. Mosques post signs on their walls with the exact times, and anyone with a computer can find local prayer times online.

In accordance with Qur'anic instruction, Muslims pray in the direction of Mecca. In the early years of Islam, Muhammad's followers prayed toward Jerusalem, the site of God's earlier dealings with Israelites and Christians. But during the Prophet's stay in Medina, he received a revelation to change the orientation: "Turn your face in the direction of the Sacred Mosque: wherever you [believers] may be, turn your faces to it" (2.144). The Sacred Mosque—the Kaaba in Mecca—is thus the direction to which all Muslims pray, no matter where they are in the world.

The word *qibla* refers to the direction toward Mecca, which varies depending on where one is in the world. In Seattle, Washington, for example, the *qibla* is 17.57 degrees east of north; in Jerusalem it is 22.81 degrees east of south; and in Hong Kong it is 15.09 degrees north of west. A very brief internet search can find the correct direction for virtually any place on earth. In many countries, hotel rooms have arrows on ceilings or on furniture to show visitors in which direction they should pray. The most remarkable place in the world for the *qibla* is Mecca itself, where worshippers pray in a circle around the Kaaba.

The Sunni *salat* sequence includes the following actions: standing and raising one's hands to the side of the face with palms toward the front; standing and holding one's hands against the body between the chest and the navel, right hand over

A sticker on a table in a hotel room in Sfax, Tunisia. The arrow, with an image of the Kaaba inside it, shows the *qibla*, the direction toward Mecca.

Women line up before early morning prayer in the courtyard of the Eyüp Mosque in Istanbul, Turkey.

of the *salat* vary from one Sunni school of legal thought to another.

During the course of assuming these positions, worshippers whisper or silently recite the prayers and Qur'anic verses that are assigned for each gesture, beginning and ending with *allahu akbar*, "Allah is great."

The Shia version of the *salat* is only slightly different.

As we will see in chapter 7, the *salat* is often a communal activity that takes place in a mosque. It is best to pray in the company of others, but because not everyone can go to the mosque, it is perfectly acceptable to pray elsewhere. Women in particular often find it difficult to go to the mosque at prayer time because of domestic duties, choosing to pray at home instead. Praying in other locations is also acceptable, so long as the space is clean and uncluttered. Often a prayer rug is brought out for that purpose. In Muslim lands it is not uncommon to see individuals praying on roadsides and sidewalks at the appointed times, or in office buildings, hotels, or other public venues when necessary. If one is unable to stand, bow, or kneel due to health reasons, one may do the *salat* legitimately sitting in a chair or a wheelchair.

left; bending down at the waist with one's torso parallel to the ground and one's hands on the knees; standing with one's hands to the side of the face and then with the hands down to one's sides; kneeling with one's forehead, nose, hands, knees, and toes on the floor; sitting on one's feet with one's hands on the knees. Depending on which *salat* is being performed, these steps are repeated as prescribed. The final act is sitting on one's feet and turning one's head to the right and then to the left while saying, *as-salamu alaykum*, "Peace be upon you," to the other worshippers. Some details

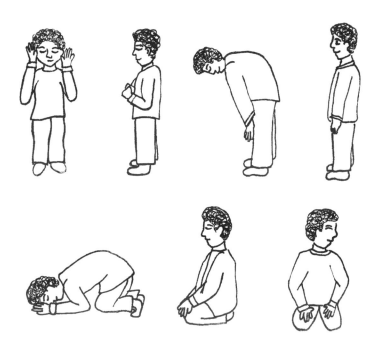

Steps in the *salat*.

Men praying the *salat* in the Umayyad Mosque in Aleppo, Syria (above). Latecomers at a crowded mosque in Akhisar, Turkey, pray individually in the street (below).

Whenever two or more people pray together, wherever they may be, one serves as the imam in front of the others. *Imam* is a word that is used in different contexts in Islam, and in this context it is the one who leads the prayer whenever two or more people are involved. If two men pray together, for example, they will not pray side by side, but one will be in front of the other to serve as imam. If only women are together for the *salat*, one will be the imam, but otherwise the imam will be a man.

We call the *salat* prayer, yet it is less of a private conversation with Allah than a ceremonial ritual in which the worshipper demonstrates submission. During the *salat* one may ask for blessings, but that kind of supplication is more commonly expressed in other contexts that we will examine in chapter 10. In addition, the *salat* has a profound influence in binding Muslims all over the world together. One can only imagine how many people around the globe, at any moment day or night, are facing one place on the planet—the Kaaba in Mecca—as a unified community of believers.

Almsgiving (*zakat*)

The *zakat* is a payment of money by individuals, traditionally about 2.5 percent of one's liquid assets, to benefit the poor. We use English terms like *alms* and *almsgiving* with reference to it, but those words are not quite accurate. The *zakat* is a religious tax, a requirement and an act of submission and worship, and it is not to be confused with kindness, charity, or generosity. Paying it fulfills an obligation to Allah. The Qur'an teaches that Allah owns "all that is in the heavens and earth" (34.1), so in giving, worshippers are not sacrificing anything of their own but are using Allah's resources to bless others.

In earlier times in Muslim countries, governments collected the *zakat* as a tax and distributed it as needed. Some governments continue to collect it today, but in countries without Muslim majorities, individuals are responsible for paying it on their own, usually at their local mosque or another charitable organization. One is allowed to select a recipient, but because the purpose is to benefit the poor, donating to other causes does not meet the *zakat*'s intent. Also, the money is intended for local needs, so givers look for opportunities in their own communities. Muslims who wish to conceal the source of the money from recipients can find ways to accomplish that.

In non-Muslim countries, Muslims have found ways to pay the *zakat* within the realities of the cultures and countries in which they live. The head of a local Islamic society in the United States provided this explanation for me:

> Even though some types of *zakat* are mandatory for Muslims, there is no requirement that they have to go through the mosques. The main goal is to see that they reach the poor people of the community. Some in our community take care of it on their own. Others do process them through the Islamic Society. We keep the *zakat* fund strictly separated from the other funds, as this money can be spent only for the poor people. We disburse these funds to the needy members of our local community. In the post 9/11 time, we strictly avoid sending this money overseas. And yes, our members can and do claim these as charitable donations on their tax returns.

The *zakat* is not the only way of giving in Islam. We will see in chapter 10 that Muslims show their generosity by means of other kinds of charitable donations.

Chapter 6

Fasting and Pilgrimage

Terms and Names to Know

Gregorian calendar, lunar (*hijri*) calendar, fast, Ramadan, Hajj, Umrah, Eid al-Adha, stoning Satan

The 365-day calendar used throughout the world—the Gregorian calendar—is based on one revolution of the earth around the sun. It is a system that fixes months to seasons and to the natural cycles of the weather, assuring, for example, that in the northern hemisphere July will always be in the summer and that December 21 will always be the shortest day of the year. Most Muslims use this calendar, as others do, for the normal aspects of their lives that require scheduling events and activities, from business to vacations to birthdays.

Islam also has a separate lunar calendar (the *hijri* calendar) that governs all of its religious dates and celebrations. The Islamic calendar has twelve months that are tied to the cycles of the moon, with each month beginning with the new moon. Depending on sunrise and sunset times, each month can have either twenty-nine or thirty days. Because the months are therefore shorter than the months in the Gregorian calendar, events tied to Islam's calendar move through the seasons about eleven days earlier each year. It takes about thirty-three years for those events to cycle through the whole solar year.

Fasting during Ramadan

Many are aware that Muslims fast for an entire month each year—during the month of Ramadan. From dawn in the morning until sunset in the evening, they abstain from normal activities that satisfy physical needs and desires—eating, drinking, and sexual relations. Observant Muslims who smoke (though some Muslims believe that smoking is always prohibited) also abstain from that during Ramadan.

Like other annual Muslim observances, Ramadan moves through the Gregorian calendar, so in some years it will be hotter, wetter, or dryer than in other years. In addition, in winter months the sun rises later and sets earlier, shortening the hours of fasting. Celebrating Ramadan in June and July will therefore be more physically taxing than during cooler, shorter winter days.

Ramadan Dates

2019	May 6–June 4
2020	April 24–May 23
2021	April 13–May 12
2022	April 3–May 2
2023	March 23–April 21
2024	March 11–April 9
2025	March 1–30
2026	February 18–March 19
2027	February 8–March 9
2028	January 28–February 26

Ramadan is an important month in Islam because in it God revealed the Qur'an: "It was in the month of Ramadan that the Qur'an was revealed as guidance for mankind, clear messages giving guidance and distinguishing between right and wrong. . . . [Allah] wants you to complete the prescribed period and to glorify Him for having guided you, so that you may be thankful" (2.185).

Fasting in this month is not only an acknowledgment of God's blessing in providing the guidance of the Qur'an, but it is also an exercise of putting spiritual concerns over physical desires. The goal in Islam is *submission*, and abstaining is evidence to God that one has truly embraced the faith. A *hadith* records Muhammad saying, "Whoever fasted the month of Ramadan out of sincere faith and hoping for a reward from Allah, then all his past sins will be forgiven" (Bukhari 2014). The blessing of forgiveness is accompanied by a special allotment of divine protection: "When the month of Ramadan starts, the gates of the heaven are opened and the gates of hell are closed and the devils are chained" (Bukhari 1899).

Islam makes accommodations for those who for a variety of reasons are not able to fast. Part of the revelation states, "Anyone who is ill or on a journey should make up for the lost days by fasting on other days later" (2.185). Exempt from the fast are those who have medical needs, including pregnant and nursing women. Islamic tradition has established rules for travelers and others to make up the lost days, but the overriding principle is that fasting is not a punishment but a blessing, and "God wants ease for you, not hardship" (2.185).

Lights decorating homes and a street in Jerusalem for Ramadan.

The month of Ramadan starts and ends with the sighting of the new moon, and at the end of each day the setting of the sun removes the restrictions. Experts in local communities observe the skies to provide official rulings, but ordinary people can also rely on published sunset times. People often turn on the radio to channels that broadcast special Qur'an recitations each evening as soon as the fast ends, but the call for prayer coming from the local mosque also announces the setting of the sun. Some communities aid in the process by announcing the sunset in more noticeable ways. In Jerusalem, for example, a blast from a cannon heard from miles away joins the sound of the call for prayer from mosques all over town. Families typically have breakfast just before dawn and a nice dinner shortly after sunset.

Ramadan is also a time for giving. Many Muslims place emphasis on charitable giving during the month of fasting.

Pilgrimage to Mecca

The pilgrimage to Mecca, the Hajj, is one of the most important features of Islam. Muslims are enjoined to go on the Hajj once in their lifetime if they are physically well and financially able to do it without going into debt. Because of the expense and the difficulty of travel, most are never in a position to make the trip. Unlike other aspects of Islam, the Hajj can be accomplished only in one place on earth, Mecca in the kingdom of Saudi Arabia, and it takes place on the same dates each year in the Islamic calendar.

Mecca was a holy city to Muslims from the beginning. Because they believe that the Kaaba was built by Abraham and Ishmael, or in some traditions by Adam and later repaired by Abraham and Ishmael, it is believed to have always been a sacred place for true religion. For Muslims it is the most important building in the world and the direction of their prayers, as we have seen. Because Muslims do not depict Allah in statues or represent him in any kind of images, let alone a building, the Kaaba serves merely as a symbol for his presence and a reminder of his oneness, majesty, and mercy.

The Hajj is a multiday ritual that includes a variety of ceremonial actions meant to draw worshippers' thoughts to divine things. It is part of Muhammad's prophetic *sunna*, and Muslims do what they do today because they are following the pattern of behavior that he first established. The Hajj is entirely participatory, and the worshipper is the one who performs the rites.

The Pilgrimage takes place each year in the Muslim month Dhu al-Hijjah, typically extending from the eighth to the thirteenth days of the month. As we saw with the month of Ramadan, the moving of the lunar months through our solar calendar means that the Hajj is about eleven days earlier each year.

Beginning Hajj Dates	
2019	August 9
2020	July 29
2021	July 18
2022	July 7
2023	June 26
2024	June 15
2025	June 5
2026	May 25
2027	May 14
2028	May 3

People travel from all over the world to experience the Hajj, and many must save for years before their dream to attend it will be realized. With about two million pilgrims each year, the logistical pressures on the government of Saudi Arabia are enormous. The Saudi kings identify themselves as "Custodians of the Two Holy Mosques" (Mecca and Medina) and are responsible to provide sufficient food, transportation, tents, toilets, water, medical services, and crowd control to make the Hajj run successfully. Unfortunately, fires in the tent city, accidental stampedes at holy sites, and outbreaks of disease have marred the experience on occasion. But given the vast numbers who attend, it continues to be an amazingly successful event.

The description that follows summarizes a typical experience that includes the two main parts—the Umrah and the Hajj.

Umrah

The Umrah is a ritual that one can undertake at any time of the year, but most people who do the Hajj do the Umrah on the same trip in the days preceding the eighth of the month or after the Hajj is completed. Before one begins, one needs to dress appropriately. Men wear two unstitched pieces of white cloth, one around the waist and one over the torso, and women wear loose clothing of their own choosing, covered except for the face and the hands.

The Umrah takes place at the Kaaba, which is in the middle of Mecca and is surrounded by Mecca's enormous Great Mosque. It has two parts. The first consists of circling around the Kaaba seven times. One does not need to touch the Kaaba, and in a huge crowd this would be impossible for most worshippers. As one walks around the ancient structure in a counterclockwise direction, one utters prayers and *suras* from the Qur'an that are prescribed for the occasion. The second part of the Umrah is a ritual that takes place nearby, still within the walls of the Great Mosque. It involves walking seven times between two hills. The hills are about 450 meters apart, so the seven walks between them will total about 3.15 kilometers. If physically able, men are expected to run part of the way.

Islam places many obligations on worshippers, but as we have seen with the *salat* and with fasting, it provides ample allowances for those who have challenges to fulfill those obligations. The circumambulation (circling around) of the Kaaba and the walk between the two hills can be accomplished in wheel chairs if needed. And the path between the two hills is in a large gallery that includes a special lane for the elderly and the disabled.

The Great Mosque in Mecca during the Hajj. Mecca is now a large city with a population of over two million. Access to the city is restricted to Muslims.

The symbolism of these activities is important. The circling of the Kaaba connects Muslims with their spiritual ancestors Abraham, Hagar, and Ishmael, who once walked on the same paths that they walk on today, and with Muhammad and the early Muslims, who did the circuit around the Kaaba just as is done now.

The walk between the two hills tells a story that is sacred to Muslim history and brings modern pilgrims into that story. Abraham's first wife, Sarah, became jealous when his wife Hagar had a baby boy, Ishmael. As a result, Abraham took Hagar and her baby away. When they arrived at the empty spot that would one day become Mecca, he left them under a tree and set out to return home. According to an important *hadith* narrated by Ibn Abbas, one of the Prophet's companions, Hagar called out: "O Abraham! To whom are you leaving us?" He replied that he was leaving them in Allah's care. Hagar had a water skin from which she drank to produce milk so she could nurse her baby. When that ran out, she ascended a nearby hill and looked, hoping to see someone to provide water for her. No one was there. In an effort to find water, she ran back and forth between the hills seven times. Then she heard a voice, and she said to the voice, "'Help us if you can offer any help.' Lo! It was Gabriel (who had made the voice). Gabriel hit the earth with his heel like this (Ibn Abbas hit the earth with his heel to illustrate it), and so the water gushed out. . . . Ishmael's mother started drinking from the water and her milk increased for her child" (Bukhari 3365).

This story narrates the beginning of Abraham's family's connection with Mecca. It provides the basis for the walking and running between the two hills in the Umrah, and it explains the origin of the Zamzam well that still produces water within the confines of Mecca's Great Mosque, about twenty meters from the Kaaba. As the *hadith* continues, we also learn the origin of the Kaaba itself. Once when Abraham was visiting Ishmael and his family in Mecca, he said, "'O Ishmael, Your Lord has ordered me to build a house for Him.' Ishmael said, 'Obey (the order of) your Lord.' Abraham said, 'Allah has also ordered me that you should help me therein.' Ishmael said, 'Then I will do'" (Bukhari 3365). The two of them built the Kaaba together. The Qur'an adds, "When Abraham and Ishmael were raising the foundations of the House, [they prayed,] 'Our Lord, accept [it] from us. Truly Thou art the Hearing, the Knowing. And, our Lord, make us submit unto Thee, and from our progeny a community submitting unto Thee" (2.127–28[N]).

Pilgrims on the Hajj.

Hajj

On the eighth day of the month Dhu al-Hijjah, pilgrims leave Mecca and travel eight kilometers to Mina. There they spend the day in prayer and worship. At Mina is located the world's largest tent city, with over a hundred thousand tents erected to house the two million pilgrims. The following day, on the ninth, they wait until dawn and then travel about fourteen kilometers to Arafat, a vast plain with a hill of the same name, also called the Mount of Mercy. This is the site of Muhammad's last sermon to pilgrims, and on this day worshippers surround the hill or sit on it in a day of praise, repentance, and prayer. After sunset, they travel nine kilometers to Muzdalifah, where they spend the night in worship.

The tenth day of the month is the important Muslim holy day Eid al-Adha. Before sunrise on this day, pilgrims leave Muzdalifah and return to Mina. They pick up pebbles at either place for the day's ritual of stoning Satan. Three large pillars have been set up in Mina. At the largest of these, the pilgrims throw seven stones in succession, each time saying "*allahu akbar*," "Allah is great." Muslim tradition holds that when God commanded Abraham to sacrifice his son Ishmael as a test of his faith, Satan tempted Abraham to disobey God's command. Abraham threw stones at him to refuse the temptation and chase Satan away. After the stoning, worshippers sacrifice an animal singularly or in conjunction with others, or they pay for a sacrifice in their behalf. This symbolizes God providing an animal for Abraham to sacrifice in place of Ishmael. Returning to Mecca, worshippers circle the Kaaba and walk between the two hills if they have not done so already. They then spend the night in Mina.

Eid al-Adha is the Feast of Sacrifice, and it is celebrated not only at the Hajj in Mina and Mecca but in mosques and homes all over the world. The Qur'an tells the story behind it: "We gave [Abraham] the good news that he would have a patient son. When the boy was old enough to work with his father, Abraham said, 'My son, I have seen myself sacrificing you in a dream. What do you think?' He said, 'Father, do as you are commanded and, God willing, you will find me steadfast.' When they had both submitted to God, and he had laid his son down on the side of his face,

We called out to him, 'Abraham, you have fulfilled the dream.' This is how We reward those who do good—it was a test to prove [their true characters]—We ransomed his son with a momentous sacrifice, and We let him be praised by succeeding generations: 'Peace be upon Abraham!'" (37.101–9).

On the remaining two days of the pilgrimage, worshippers continue in prayer, praise, and contemplation at Mina. Each afternoon, they stone Satan symbolically at each of the three pillars—seven stones in succession, each accompanied by "*allahu akbar.*" The stoning of the second pillar is said to represent Hagar's rejection of Satan's temptation for her to stop the sacrifice, and the stoning of the third is said to represent Ishmael's rejection of Satan's efforts to dissuade him from participating. For all the individual pilgrims, these activities are meant as reminders to strengthen their own resolve to withstand the temptations that they are faced with today.

After pilgrims have finished at Mina, they return to Mecca. There, before they leave the holy city, they perform a farewell series of circuits around the Kaaba, and with that their pilgrimage is completed. Many are not ready to fly home from Mecca at that point, however. Though not part of the Hajj and not mandatory, many pilgrims then travel to Medina and visit the tomb of Muhammad.

A home in Jerusalem decorated with symbols that show that the occupants have participated in the Hajj. One who has participated in the Hajj is often called by the honorific title *Hajji* (for a man), or *Hajja* (for a woman).

Chapter 7
The Mosque

Muslims form an international community, the *umma*, a vast body of believers. Although they are found throughout the world, most still live in Muslim-majority countries or in Muslim-majority environments within countries that have large Muslim populations. This situation has changed dramatically in recent decades with the migration of millions out of traditionally Muslim nations. Mosques, whether in Islamic homelands or in countries where Muslims are scarce, provide not only a place to pray but also an anchor for a community of believers.

Place of Prayer

Likely the most visible and recognizable evidence of Islam is the mosque. The word *mosque*, Arabic *masjid*, means "place of prostration," that is, "bowing-down place." Technically, any place set aside specifically for prayer, whether it has a roof over it or not, is a mosque as long as it has a defined border around it that sets it apart from the

ordinary world. In Islam's earliest history in Arabia, mosques were outdoor places where people came together to perform the *salat*. The earliest mosque structures in Medina were courtyards with walls around them, often partially covered to provide protection from the sun during prayers. As the *umma* began to grow and Muslims moved to, or were converted in, places more prone to rain and snow, it became necessary to construct more elaborate architectural spaces for worship.

The main features of mosques are remarkably consistent around the world. A large mosque will have a tower called a *minaret*, or two or more of them. Smaller mosques, or buildings converted into mosques, may have none. The minaret provides a high venue from which to broadcast the call for worshippers to come to pray, but it also serves a decorative function that adds character and beauty to the building.

Because the prayer hall is space deliberately separated from the ordinary world that surrounds it, one does not wear one's shoes there. Most

The Islamic Society of Boston Cultural Center in Boston, Massachusetts, USA, has a tall minaret and a dome over the prayer hall.

mosques have space inside the door where one removes one's shoes and places them on designated shelves. In mosques where the outside doors lead directly into the prayer hall, one removes one's shoes before entering the building.

The prayer hall is a large single room. Based on local architecture, this hall may be a forest of columns or an open room, sometimes under a central dome. One's eyes are drawn to a wall at the front. The mosque is built so this wall is perpendicular to the *qibla*, the direction to Mecca, meaning that wherever one is in the mosque, when one faces that wall one is facing Mecca. Except in very poor and humble mosques, the floor is covered with carpet. In a well-funded mosque, the floor may be covered with a single carpet with a repeating pattern that may look like many smaller rugs. In villages, sometimes small individual rugs cover the floor, often donated by local worshippers.

On the main wall of the prayer hall will typically be two important features. In the middle of the wall there will be a niche that often looks somewhat like a narrow fireplace. This is called the *mihrab*. Its function is to identify the *qibla*. To the right of it there is usually a ceremonial staircase called the *minbar*. It is a lectern used for special readings and sermons. Mosques never contain statues or paintings as are found in many Christian churches. Sometimes mosques are decorated with geometric or vegetal designs, and often they showcase beautiful calligraphy with the names of Allah, Muhammad, the Rightly Guided Caliphs (in Sunni mosques), or with important Islamic phrases. The poorest mosques cannot afford those but usually have phrases hanging in frames or even painted on the walls.

As new Muslim communities develop around the world, Muslims often cannot afford to build mosques until they can raise sufficient funds. They thus purchase existing buildings and remodel them to meet their needs. Because those buildings are not built with a wall perpendicular to the *qibla* and sometimes do not have a *mihrab*, Muslims make do with what they have by hanging

The Mamluk-period al-Ashraf Barsbay Mosque in Cairo, Egypt, was built in 1423. At the center of the wall that shows the *qibla* is the niche called the *mihrab*, beautifully crafted in different colors of stone. The combination of black, red, and white stone in the arches is seen frequently in Mamluk architecture. The wooden *minbar* is original and incorporates different colors of inlaid wood and ivory.

something on the wall to serve as a *qibla* marker. Sometimes the carpet in these renovated buildings will have lines on it that do not align with the building itself but show worshippers where to line up and in what direction to pray. To meet the needs of travelers, in the Islamic world there are truck-stop mosques attached to gas stations, and there are even mosques in malls and airports.

Women and men pray separately in the mosque in order to avoid distraction during worship. Larger mosques have a balcony where women pray, or a space on the side or in the back, separated by a barrier. Because of the physical movements undertaken in the *salat*, it is considered unseemly for women to be seen praying in front of men.

The leader of a mosque is called the *imam*. This is our second meaning of the word, the first being the individual who serves temporarily to lead in the *salat*. The imam who oversees the mosque usually occupies a paid position. He has special education and training, and in some countries he is employed by the state. He oversees the building and its services and assures that all is done in accordance with the Qur'an and the *sunna*. While it is desirable to have a full-time trained imam, members of a small community that cannot afford one can build a mosque on their own and carry on with worship by selecting a knowledgeable member of the congregation to lead prayers. Mosques are often organizationally independent of the other mosques in the area.

Prayer (*salat*)

We were introduced to the *salat* in chapter 5. Several different activities take place in a mosque, but its primary function is to be a location for

Women praying individually in the Yeni Cami (New Mosque) in Istanbul, Turkey. The women's area is separated from the rest of the prayer hall by a screen that gives the women relative privacy while they participate in the *salat*.

An increasingly uncommon sight is a muezzin up in a minaret announcing a live call to prayer. Most *adhan*s are now broadcast from loudspeakers with the muezzin inside the building using a microphone. This photograph was taken in Bergama, Turkey, in 1983.

communal prayer. To gather worshippers to the *salat*, whether in a city or in a small village, a man called the *muezzin* recites the call to prayer, known as the *adhan*, about ten to twenty minutes before each scheduled prayer time. Presented below is a translation of the Sunni version of the *adhan*. The Shia version, which we will see in chapter 9, differs in some wording from this.

> Allah is great (*four times*).
> I testify that there is no god but Allah (*twice*).
> I testify that Muhammad is the Messenger of Allah (*twice*).
> Come to prayer (*twice*).
> Come to salvation and prosperity (*twice*).
> Prayer is better than sleep (*twice, morning prayer only*).
> Allah is great (*twice*).
> There is no god but Allah.

The *adhan* was established in Muhammad's time and continues today from mosques around the world. In earlier times, the muezzin called the *adhan* by climbing a minaret and reciting the call from there. In modern days it is usually broadcast from loudspeakers on the minaret, sometimes from a muezzin with a microphone inside the mosque and sometimes from a recording. Even to many non-Muslims, the sound of the *adhan* is strikingly beautiful and impressive, especially in big cities where the calls do not start at the same moment and come from different voices and from different directions all over town.

As worshippers arrive at the mosque to join in the *salat*, they first wash themselves before entering the prayer hall: "Believers, when you rise to pray wash your faces and your hands as far as the elbow, and wipe your heads and your feet to the ankle" (5.6). This ritual washing is called *wudu*. Sometimes there is a row of faucets on the side of the mosque near the entrance, with benches or seats for worshippers to sit on while they do the ceremonial washing. Often the washing facility is inside the door of the mosque but before one enters the

Worshippers perform the *wudu*, the ritual washing, prior to entering the Yeni Cami (New Mosque) in Istanbul, Turkey.

prayer hall. This ceremonial washing is an important part of ritual prayer that represents becoming cleansed prior to entering the sacred space.

If a worshipper has come to pray in response to the call to prayer, he or she will be part of a group that prays in unison, often with many others. Worshippers line up in straight lines facing the wall that shows the *qibla*. As more men arrive, they fill in the line from one side of the hall to the other, then a second line behind the first, and so on. Meanwhile, women are lining up in the same way in the women's section. There will always be an imam leading the prayer in front of the other worshippers, no matter how many are praying.

Mosques around the world are sometimes among the most beautiful buildings in any location. Reflecting local architectural influences as well as climate realities, they are often recognizable because of their distinctive styles. For example, North African mosques often have a single bulky minaret; Turkish mosques have thin, round minarets (frequently more than one); and Indonesian mosques are often quite colorful. In areas where Muslims are a minority, such as Europe and North America, mosques frequently reflect the styles of the homelands of the Muslims who built them and worship in them. Sometimes, however, they reflect local architectural tastes instead.

Prayer hall of the King Abdullah Mosque, Amman, Jordan. This modern mosque retains many of the traditional features of older mosques, including a large dome over the prayer hall, stained glass windows, and a large chandelier. New mosques often employ modern architecture, but they always include the most important elements of the mosque—a place for the ritual washing (*wudu*) and a prayer hall with a *mihrab*.

Other Functions of the Mosque

Mosques have purposes other than prayer, and those vary based on the needs of the local Muslim community. Often the mosque serves as the local community center. Sometimes when children attend secular public schools, the mosque serves as a venue for religion classes, often held on Sunday. Thus mosques in non-Muslim countries may include classrooms. In addition, mosques often serve as a convenient location for local people to rest or eat lunch, and in big cities there are almost always men taking afternoon naps. Once while traveling in Turkey, I grew ill and was very thankful to be able to spend an afternoon lying on the carpeted floor of a six-hundred-year-old Ottoman mosque.

Islam does not have a sabbath like Judaism, but on Fridays there is a special community prayer called the *jumma*. Because attending the *jumma* is obligatory for men, it is the most well-attended prayer of the week. It takes place early in the afternoon, and it is accompanied by a sermon delivered by the imam or, in smaller congregations, by a local respected Muslim.

Mosques have traditionally been located in the center of the local population, and around them are found conveniences that benefit worshippers and others. Public lavatories are often nearby, as well as water fountains and venues for food. Mosques in larger communities are almost always accompanied by nearby stores that sell Islamic paraphernalia, such as books, prayer beads, head scarves, other *hijab* clothing, wall hangings or posters of the mosques in Mecca and Medina, posters of Qur'an passages in beautiful calligraphy, and even posters of favorite preachers or Qur'an reciters.

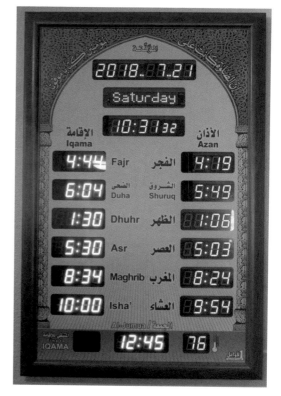

Posted prayer times at the Masjid Ikhlas in Denver, Colorado, USA. The automated display allows the times to be updated electronically daily. Notice that the *adhan* times are shown in the right column.

The modern world has caught up with mosque worship just as it has with other aspects of ordinary and religious life. In addition to the use of microphones and loud speakers, prayer times are sometimes shown on LED displays, and "Turn off your mobile phone" signs are now a common sight at entrances to mosques.

on earth to the whims of mortals but has set in place a system by which all can recognize those he has chosen. History is divided into two periods—the era of prophecy and the era of interpretation. The dividing line between the two periods was the death of Muhammad, when prophecy ended. Shia Muslims believe in divinely chosen and guided leaders whom they call *imams*. (This is our third meaning of the word *imam*, the others applying to prayer leaders and mosque leaders.) The Shia take their imams very seriously, believing that they have authority from Allah to interpret his word that was revealed to Muhammad during the era of prophecy.

The first imam was Ali himself, and the rest were his descendants—descendants of Ali and his wife Fatima, Muhammad's daughter. Thus the Shia list their first three imams as Ali, Ali's son Hasan, and then Ali's son Husayn.

We saw in chapter 3 that not long after Ali became caliph, an army of Arabs attacked him in the Battle of the Camel. In Shia memory that became one of many injustices committed by the Sunnis against the Shia imams. Ali prevailed but had to contend next with Muawiya, who would later be the founder of the Umayyad dynasty. Because Ali chose to negotiate rather than fight, he was murdered by a member of a Muslim extremist group, the Kharijites that we met in chapter 3.

Ali and Fatima's son Hasan succeeded his father as caliph but was forced to surrender his position to Muawiya after only six months. When he died, supporters of the family wanted his brother Husayn to be the caliph. When Husayn was traveling from Mecca to Mesopotamia in 680, the armies of Muawiya's successor ambushed his caravan at a place called Karbala. There Umayyad soldiers killed him and many of his family members. They cut off his head and took it to Damascus as a trophy. There is a shrine for it there in the Great Mosque and another one at the al-Husayn Mosque in Cairo, with competing accounts of where the head is now. (Another account has Husayn's head being brought back to Karbala to join his body in his tomb there.)

Husayn's martyrdom at the Battle of Karbala, viewed as Sunni treachery against Ali's family, is one of the key events in Shia history and is memorialized every year.

Shia Fundamentals

The foregoing history was necessary because much of what Shia do and believe has to do with these historical events and their consequences. After Husayn, nine other imams followed in succession for a total of twelve altogether, each descending from Muhammad through Fatima

Shia display images of their martyred imams, including Imam Ali (left) and Imam Husayn (right).

and Ali. The majority of Shia acknowledge all twelve, and thus they are called "Twelvers." They are found most notably in Iran, southern Iraq, and Lebanon, and there are pockets in other locations around the Middle East and South Asia. In the year 874, the Twelfth Imam disappeared and went into what the Shia call "occultation," which is a mystical state of hiding. Twelvers hold that he is still alive but is hidden from the world. When Allah wills it, the Twelfth Imam will return to public view as the *mahdi*, an eschatological figure who will usher in an era of peace and happiness before the judgment day.

A different group, the Ismailis, makes up less than ten percent of the Shia population. Located today mostly in India, the Ismailis are followers of the Seventh Imam, Ismail, who died before he became imam and is believed to have taken the position with him into heaven. Thus they are called "Seveners" because they believe that the line of imams ended with the seventh. Ismail will return at the end of time as the *mahdi*.

The Zaidis, an even smaller division, recognize a different Fifth Imam from the one recognized by Twelvers and Seveners. Today they make up about 40 percent of the population of Yemen.

The Druze religion—found primarily in Syria, Lebanon, and northern Israel—broke away from the Ismailis a thousand years ago yet is often considered not to be part of Islam.

Like Sunnis, Shia believe that prophecy ended with Muhammad. But the Shia ascribe spiritual powers and wisdom to their imams far beyond what Sunnis ascribe to anyone but the Prophet himself. The twelve imams provided guidance for the Shia community in the same way that Muhammad did, though without the revelation of a book containing Allah's words. When the Twelfth Imam went into occultation, the guidance of the community did not end with him but continued in the hands of the Shia legal scholars, the *ulama*, who now continue his mission as earthly imams. Thus in Shiism, the *ulama* are the inheritors and continuers of the process of divine guidance. In addition, at least in recent decades, some of the Shia clergy have asserted that their learning and the tradition which they continue should give them political power as well, so in the

The Mosque of Imam Ali in Najaf, Iraq, a destination for Shia pilgrims from around the world. Mosques containing tombs of the imams and their family members are found in several locations, mostly in Iraq and Iran.

Islamic Republic of Iran, ultimate authority rests in the hands of scholars.

The authority of the Shia clergy is based on two important factors: their knowledge of the law, and the doctrinal principle that Allah continues to provide leadership through earthly representatives. Through their advanced training, academic reputations, and other achievements, scholars ascend through various ranks to arrive at the highest stations within the *ulama*, such as ayatollah (meaning "Sign of Allah") and grand ayatollah. In Iran and Iraq, these men often have large followings, and believers select the ones they prefer and pray at their mosques.

Shia Worship Practices

The Shia system of worship includes deeply emotional religious participation and the intense veneration of important people. The Shia have built elaborate mosques around the tombs of their imams and their imams' family members. Foremost are the tombs of Ali at Najaf and Husayn at Karbala, both in modern Iraq. These and other shrines attract millions of pilgrims who pray at the tombs, weeping loudly and showing their grief demonstrably as they remember the martyrdoms of their beloved heroes.

The tomb of Sayyida Ruqayya in Damascus, Syria. Ruqayya was a little girl when her father, Imam Husayn, was killed in the Battle of Karbala. The Umayyads took her to Damascus, where, according to Shia tradition, she soon died of a broken heart. Shia visit the site with great emotion, and some place dolls and other gifts on top of Ruqayya's tomb.

Many Sunnis consider these emotional observances to be highly inappropriate, if not evidence of polytheism, because they involve the veneration of humans rather than of Allah alone. But for the Shia, the connection they have with Allah's chosen imams, descendants of the Prophet himself, are at the core of their understanding of Islam.

Shia accept the Qur'an, pray toward Mecca, attend the Hajj there, say the *shahada*, fast during Ramadan, hear the call to prayer, go to the mosque, do the *salat*, pay the *zakat*, celebrate the holy days, and do most other Islamic things quite like the Sunnis do them. There are differences, however, in many of the details. The Shia *adhan* (call to prayer) differs from that of the Sunnis with the inclusion of the phrase "I testify that Ali is the vicegerent of Allah." In the Shia *salat* worshippers position their hands a little

differently and say some different words. They do not put their foreheads on the carpet but on a small disk of baked clay to remind them that they came from the earth. As for the *sunna*, the Shia have different collections of *hadith* that favor traditions that were passed down through Ali, and they also consider as authoritative the teachings and practices of their imams. Shia have been less reticent than Sunnis to make images of people, and Shia artwork through the centuries has sometimes included images showing Muhammad's face. Shia do not hesitate to publish and display pictures of Ali, Husayn, or their favorite ayatollahs.

The observance that probably shows the Shia-Sunni divide most graphically is Ashura, in which the Shia recall the Battle of Karbala when Imam Husayn was killed by the Sunni Umayyads. Somber processions mark the day, with worshippers walking and mourning together and with thousands visiting the shrine of Husayn. One practice that used to be more common than it is now involves worshippers pounding their chests, whipping themselves, or even cutting their heads with blades. By doing this, they are showing their oneness with Husayn and his suffering and expressing their grief that they were not there to help him. Nowadays, activities of this sort are not universally sanctioned as appropriate by Shia authorities. Iran's religious establishment has prohibited the practice of cutting and has encouraged worshippers to donate blood instead.

Another manifestation of Ashura is the *taziya*. In Iran and Iraq the term refers to a "passion play" of Husayn's martyrdom, perhaps performed by amateur actors in a town square or narrated by a storyteller. There are many varieties in the observance. In south Asia, people carry a portable model of Husayn's tomb through the streets in remembrance.

In recalling the deaths of Ali, Husayn, and others of Muhammad's family, Shia Muslims see evidence of moral victory in the face of worldly injustice and tyranny. This in itself is not out of harmony with the early career of Muhammad

A *turba* is a small disk of baked clay used by Shia when performing the *salat*, signifying the soil of the earth. The forehead of the worshipper is placed on the *turba* instead of on the floor, showing one's connection to the earth out of which humans were created. Many of these disks are made from the soil of Karbala, the site of Imam Husayn's death. Sayyida Ruqayya Mosque, Damascus, Syria.

and the earliest *sura*s of the Qur'an, which show a minority religious group in struggle with surrounding forces, facing great odds and prevailing in the end.

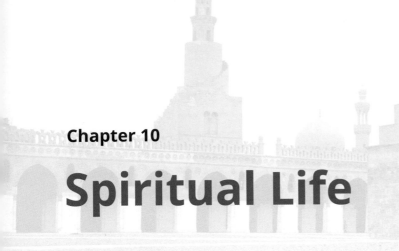

Chapter 10

Spiritual Life

Terms and Names to Know

taqwa, Sufism, Sufi, *dhikr*, al-Junayd, al-Ghazali, Rumi, Mevlevis, *eid*, Eid al-Fitr, Eid al-Adha, *dua*, *sadaqa*, prayer beads, popular religion, saint, *baraka*

An important aspect of a Muslim's life is *taqwa*, which can be translated as "God consciousness" or "God mindfulness." Believers are encouraged to have Allah and the things of Allah always on their minds. Adherents of any religion can attest that this is not always easy, and it requires deliberate effort. Spiritual reminders—tangible and visible items that draw one's thoughts to Allah—can be helpful in this effort.

Islam has many features that remind believers of the duties of their religion. Foods or activities that are *halal* or *haram* are daily reminders. The clothing one wears is a reminder. Observant Muslims often have hanging on the walls of their homes pictures of the Great Mosque of Mecca and the Kaaba or of a local mosque, or framed images of Qur'an passages or the *basmala*, "*In the name of Allah, the Compassionate, the Merciful.*" They hear the call to prayer five times a day from the neighborhood mosque and say the *basmala* before activities in which they desire

divine favor. Believers attend Friday prayers, observe holy days, go to the mosque, and fast during Ramadan. In addition, they use Islamic phrases in everyday speech, such as *insha allah* and *al-hamdu li-llah*.

Radio stations in Muslim lands broadcast Qur'an recitations, and believers can buy religious music in stores or stream it online. Some Muslim converts in North America wear traditional Middle Eastern clothing as a sign of their Islamic identity, even though many people in the Middle East wear the same kind of clothing that Europeans and Americans wear.

In Muslim-majority areas, one can see reminders in many places if one is observant. Cars and trucks are sometimes decorated with Islamic images such as pictures of mosques or prayer beads hanging over rearview mirrors. One can sometimes see the word *Allah* written on the walls of buildings or on other public venues. Displays like these show the commitment of

A drinking fountain in Damascus, Syria, reminding passersby to always remember God.

worshippers to their faith, but they also provide welcome reminders to help them in their quest for *taqwa*.

Inside a Palestinian taxi driver's car, a Qur'an and pictures of Jerusalem's two great Islamic landmarks—the al-Aqsa Mosque and the Dome of the Rock.

Sufism

Sufism is Islamic mysticism, and a Sufi is an Islamic mystic. Sufism has a long history, but many modern Muslims do not know much about it. It is worth discussing, however, because it has been important historically, it continues to thrive, and it teaches us something about the human quest for contact with the Divine.

Mystics in any religious tradition are usually those who feel that there is something beyond the outward practices of religion and who search for a more spiritual experience. It is a quest that many Muslims have undertaken for an inner, deeper spiritual life than what they feel they can obtain through the normal worship practices of Islam. They do not abandon those formal observances, but they believe that there is more to be had. Sufism has been described as "the inner dimension of the Sharia" that comes through "abandoning oneself to Allah." For some the model, in an ultimate but abstract sense, is Muhammad's Night Journey and Ascension into heaven. Like other mystic endeavors, Sufism sometimes includes asceticism—self-denial with respect to material possessions and comforts. The way to Sufi fulfillment is thus not always easy, but the goal is setting aside the worldly for the heavenly, something that the Qur'an itself makes desirable for all believers.

Sufis are organized in "orders"—societies or communities in which one learns how to live the mystical life. Sufi societies have people in training as well as experienced masters, with chains of predecessors that connect today's master with masters of the past. The communities vary in their nature, and often they involve practitioners who have jobs and families and live otherwise ordinary lives while meeting regularly with their Sufi brothers. In some cases, a religious men's club is a better analogy than a monastery, though many Sufi orders have been residential communities.

A tree next to the Muhammad Ali Mosque in Cairo, Egypt, with *Allah* sculpted into the leaves and branches.

Sufis achieve and express their spirituality by means of *dhikr* (sometimes spelled *zikr*), a word meaning "remembering" or "mentioning." The *dhikr* is a specific ritual activity that Sufis undertake in order to arrive at a state of mental and spiritual disconnect from earthly surroundings and obtain temporary union with Allah. Examples include such things as Qur'an recitation, music, dance, and chanting "Allah" or "There is no god but Allah." Many *dhikr*s do not seem out of the ordinary except for the extent to which the Sufis take them—often very long-lasting, rhythmic repetitions. Sometimes words or phrases are chanted hundreds of times in a row. An easy internet video search for "Sufi dhikr" can provide multiple examples. Although activities of this sort may seem strange to some, the goal is not much different from that of the ecstatic singing of Christian Pentecostals or even Christian rock music—obtaining spirituality by losing oneself in sound and rhythm.

Throughout history, many Sufis have lived in accordance with the Sharia and have been respected by others. Today there are conservative varieties of Islam in which Sufism is viewed as a dangerous innovation that seeks contact with Allah that is not permitted to any but the prophets. They find heretical the use of music, dance, and similar practices in worship. This is the position of the Wahhabis in Saudi Arabia, the widespread Salafi movement, and other groups. But among mainstream Sunnis, there has been a resurgence of the practice in recent years as many Muslims are seeking greater spiritual connections in life, believing that "God guides whoever He will to His Light" (24.35).

Three Important Sufis

A brief look at three influential Sufis from early centuries will illustrate something of the quest for this kind of spirituality.

Al-Junayd, a respected Sufi master in Baghdad (died 910), taught "annihilation" of self to achieve life with Allah. It is this "annihilation" that is the goal of various kinds of *dhikr*, annihilation of one's earthly nature to achieve renewal of self through an experience with the Divine. Al-Junayd is especially important historically because most Sufis after his time traced their spiritual lineage

from master to master and eventually to him. He is thus sometimes called the "Master of Masters."

Abu-Hamid al-Ghazali (1058–1111) was from Persia and was a religion professor in Baghdad, where he achieved fame and was very influential. He was a master of doctrine and philosophy and published important works, including *The Incoherence of the Philosophers*. In that book he argued against using philosophical tools to describe Islam and against certain beliefs that were derived through reason, including that the resurrection would be spiritual, not bodily. One of the fascinating things about al-Ghazali is how his life went through different stages with interesting career changes. The final stage of his career was that of a Sufi master of great importance.

In his professional accomplishments in Baghdad, al-Ghazali did not find the satisfaction he desired, and he sometimes felt condemned by Allah. His autobiographical description of his quest for spirituality is a thoughtful introspection.

> It had already become clear to me that I had no hope of the bliss of the world to come save through a God-fearing life and the withdrawal of myself from vain desire. . . . I considered the circumstances of my life, and realized that I was caught in a veritable thicket of attachments. I also considered my activities, of which the best was my teaching and lecturing, and realized that in them I was dealing with sciences that were unimportant and contributed nothing to the attainment of eternal life. After that I examined my motive in my work of teaching, and realized that it was not a pure desire for the things of God, but that the impulse moving me was the desire for an influential position and public recognition. (*Deliverance from Error*, in W. M. Watt, *The Faith and Practice of al-Ghazālī*, 58–59)

The professor came to some realizations about his successful life that caused him to question the very nature of success. Rather than bringing him freedom or satisfaction, his accomplishments had actually made him a prisoner. As he looked closely at his motives, he did not like what he saw, and he finally realized that he "was on the brink of a crumbling bank of sand" and would fall unless he changed the direction of his life. He would need to leave what he was doing and start a new path in pursuit of Allah, but the "thicket of attachments" in which he was trapped would make that very difficult.

> One day I would form the resolution to quit Baghdad and get rid of these adverse circumstances; the next day I would abandon my resolution. I put one foot forward and drew the other back. If in the morning I had a genuine longing to seek eternal life, by the evening the attack of a whole host of desires had reduced it to impotence. Worldly desires were striving to keep me by their chains just where I was, while the voice of faith was calling, "To the road! to the road! What is left of life is but little and the journey before you is long. All that keeps you busy, both intellectually and practically, is but hypocrisy and delusion. If you do not prepare *now* for eternal life, when will you prepare? If you do not now sever these attachments, when will you sever them?" (Ghazali, in Watt, 59)

Al-Ghazali finally quit his professorship, traveled for years, and eventually returned to his homeland in Persia. He set up a Sufi center there and was influential in spreading his newly found spirituality through his writings and teaching. One of his enduring metaphors for describing the mystic life is the comparison between a physician and a healthy person. The physician may know everything *about* health, but the healthy person *lives* health. So also, a practitioner of the spiritual life knows through experience what an academic who just studies and describes it can only know secondarily. The spiritual life cannot be comprehended by study "but only by immediate experience (*dhawq*—literally 'tasting'). . . . I apprehended clearly that the mystics were men who had real experiences, not men of words, and that I had already progressed as far as was possible by way of intellectual apprehension. What remained for me was not to be attained by . . . instruction and study but only by immediate experience and by walking in the mystic way" (Ghazali, in Watt, 57–58).

Our third Sufi master, Jalal al-Din Rumi, was born in Afghanistan in 1207 and died in Anatolia in 1273. After his own journey through life, he ended up as a Sufi master presiding over an order in Konya, now in central Turkey. Rumi wrote much poetry and even today is usually considered the most widely read poet in the world. To

The *dhikr* of a Mevlevi Sufi ("whirling dervish") in Konya, Turkey. Notice the upward and downward position of his hands.

achieve the mystical state he desired, he developed a *dhikr* based on ecstatic whirling in circles, and thus his followers are sometimes called "whirling dervishes." His Sufi order, the Mevlevis, still exists today, despite opposition from the Turkish government much of the time since the 1920s. To repetitive music, the Mevlevi Sufis spin in circles to disconnect themselves from their surroundings and focus on Allah. In imitation of the order of the universe, they circle around the master in the center, and as they spin with outstretched arms, one hand opens upward to receive divine blessings and the other opens downward to dispense the blessings to others.

Holy Days

The observance of holy days is one way ordinary Muslims maintain "God consciousness." Holy days are found throughout the year, though how they are commemorated varies from place to place and from family to family. Muhammad's birthday is of special interest, and other important commemorations include the Islamic new year, the day of Muhammad's Night Journey and Ascension, and Ashura—when some Sunnis recall the Israelites being saved from Pharaoh and when Shia recall the death of Imam Husayn at Karbala. Shia holy days also include the birth and death days of their imams and the day on which Muhammad designated Ali as his successor.

Two days on the calendar are the most important ones for Islamic observance. The first, Eid al-Fitr, is associated with Ramadan. *Eid* means "festival" or "feast," and this *eid* is the "Feast of Breaking the Fast." It takes place the day after Ramadan ends, and on that day it is strictly forbidden to fast. Muslims observe Eid al-Fitr by putting on their best clothes and attending a special early morning prayer. They then may exchange gifts with friends and family members, visit the graves of ancestors, have family gatherings, or do other worthy things that remind them of their obligations to Allah.

Eid al-Adha, the Feast of Sacrifice, comes during the period of the Hajj. Across the world, Muslims celebrate this *eid* by dressing in their best clothing, exchanging gifts, and attending special early-morning prayers at the mosque. If families can afford it, they sacrifice a sheep or a goat, or maybe even a cow or a camel. (Cows and camels can be sacrifices that are shared between families.) Part of the meat goes to the family, part to friends or extended family, and part to the poor. In the modern world, it is difficult for worshippers, especially those who live in cities and do not own livestock, to sacrifice the animals themselves. Instead, they buy the animal, and a local butcher does the slaughtering, preferably in the presence of the one bringing the sacrifice. Like Eid al-Fitr, this *eid* is a time for family gatherings and for food as well. As with those who celebrate it on the Hajj in Mecca, this holy day is meant to tie worshippers to the great stories of Abraham and his family and teach Muslims everywhere to show the same faith and submission to Allah that Abraham had.

Dua

In the Qur'an Allah says, "Call on Me and I will answer you" (40.60), and Muhammad is reported to have said, "There is nothing more honorable with Allah than supplication," which is "the essence of worship" (al-Tirmidhi 3370, 3371). *Dua* is a personal and private prayer to Allah in which an individual asks for blessings. Unlike the *salat*, it is not a ritual, nor does it involve a set pattern of movements or words, though Muslims often kneel or raise their hands. It is usually uttered silently.

Muslims believe that *dua*, as a personal supplication to Allah, brings the requested blessing if the worshipper is sincere and has good intentions and if the blessing is Allah's will. Worshippers may use their own words, and many also use phrases from the Qur'an or prayers that Muhammad uttered that are contained in the *hadith*, of which there are many examples.

> "O Allah, grant us good in this world and the good in the Hereafter, and save us from the torment of Hell-Fire." (Muslim 2690a)

> "O Allah, I seek refuge in Thee from incapacity, from indolence, from cowardice, from senility, from miserliness, and I seek refuge in Thee from

A Jerusalem apartment building with Allah written on the wall in brick.

the torment of the grave and from trial of the life and death." (Muslim 2706a)

Muhammad taught:

When you go to bed, perform ablution as is done for prayer; then lie down on the right side and recite: "O Allah, I turn my face towards Thee and entrust my affair to Thee. I retreat unto Thee for protection with hope in Thee and fear of Thee. There is no resort and no deliverer (from hardship) but Thou only. I affirm my faith in Thy books which Thou revealed and in Thine Apostles whom Thou sent." (Muslim 2710a)

Muhammad's *dua* supplications cover a wide variety of situations, so Muslims have many readily available for circumstances like seeking forgiveness, going to bed, getting up, eating, dealing with difficulties, and praying for rain. In addition, later writers composed their own *duas*, and several volumes are in print that allow Muslims a multitude of options.

Fasting

We have already seen how observant Muslims fast for the entire month of Ramadan. In addition, they are encouraged to fast on other occasions as well, not as an obligatory act but as a voluntary sign of one's submission to Allah. Such a fast is a means of increasing self-control and overcoming temptation. It is "a shield against the Fire" (ibn Majah 1639), but it is also a means of obtaining forgiveness and achieving God consciousness. Fasting on certain days is more laudatory than on others. Monday and Thursday fasts bring particular blessings, as does fasting during the middle days of each month.

Voluntary Giving (*sadaqa*)

The *zakat*, which we saw in chapter 5, is obligatory giving that one does as an obligation to Allah. Islam has another kind of giving that is voluntary and can be considered an act of charity and generosity. The word used for it is *sadaqa*, "righteousness," or "righteous act." Muhammad said that "every act of goodness is *sadaqa*" (Muslim 1005), but the righteous act for which the word has special application is the act of giving from one's possessions, which is normally done through the donation of money. The Qur'an admonishes charitable giving: "You who believe, give charitably from the good things you have acquired and that We have produced for you from the earth" (2.267). It teaches that our wealth will be a test for us and that being charitable helps protect us from our own greed (64.15–16).

Unlike the *zakat*, which is normally paid annually and is often administered by the mosque or by a larger Islamic organization, the *sadaqa* offering can be made whenever the believer sees a need and wants to help. There is a close association with this kind of giving and the fast during Ramadan, when voluntary giving is especially common. Islam's other holy days are also times of giving, and many Muslim families make giving part of their observance on those days. There is no minimal monetary requirement, and believers may give as much as they feel comfortable giving, and they give where they feel it will help. They may do so privately and individually, or they can contribute to established charitable organizations. Several Islamic charities provide facilities on the internet for making donations.

Prayer Beads

Prayer beads are historically associated with Sufis and are a traditional *dhikr* tool. But they are most often seen with people who aren't Sufis at all. Walking down the street, one can frequently see men with prayer beads in their hands, thumbing through the beads one by one. Most may just be expending nervous energy, but the design of the beads reveals their intended purpose. Most have the following pattern: eleven beads, then a bead of a different shape that serves as a divider, then eleven more beads, then a divider, then eleven more. The total is thirty-three. Tradition holds that Allah has ninety-nine names that embody his attributes, and as a *dhikr* tool, each name can be uttered with the thumbing of each consecutive bead, three times through the strand. Longer strands of ninety-nine can also be seen, divided into three groups of thirty-three each. The beads can serve in the process of *dua* or with the repetition of Qur'anic verses or prayers. Muhammad taught the virtue of repetition of praises to Allah, and some Muslims follow the pattern of repeating

Prayer beads from Aleppo, Syria.

"Glory to Allah," "Praise be to Allah," and "Allah is great" thirty-three times each. Not surprisingly, mechanical and electronic counters are now available to assist in the process, including prayer-bead apps for mobile phones.

Popular Religion and the Tombs of Saints

In most religions there is a phenomenon that scholars call "popular religion," manifestations of spirituality that are not officially sanctioned but are widespread and are considered by ordinary people to be part of their own religious observance. One such manifestation is the veneration of those who are considered "saints"—people who were remarkable for their piety and good works and whose tombs attract reverent visits even today. The Arabic term for such a person is *wali*. We were introduced to this word in chapter 9. In this context, it connotes a "friend of Allah." Shia

and most Sunnis have no trouble with the veneration of important deceased Muslims through the building of tombs and shrines, nor with honoring them through pilgrimages and prayers at their burial places. Such activities, they believe, are a means of coming closer to Allah by drawing from the spiritual power, called *baraka*, of saintly people, as well as learning from their examples and accomplishments. Many of the practitioners of this kind of veneration are women, for whom some of the *walis* have special importance for dealing with issues such as trouble conceiving children.

Because the Qur'an does not mention practices of this sort, some Sunnis consider such attention paid to humans to be a form of polytheism or *shirk*, venerating people with feelings that should be reserved for Allah alone. The Wahhabis and the Salafis are examples of modern groups that reject any kind of monument-building or pilgrimage to the tombs of the deceased, Muhammad sometimes being the exception.

Sufi masters are perhaps more likely than others to be venerated at their tombs, in large part because in life they had disciples, and those disciples had disciples who walked in their path in the generations afterward. But many other people have been honored with tombs and with visitors even centuries after their deaths. A site called Nabi Musa in Palestine is believed to hold the tomb of the prophet Moses, and each year there is a pilgrimage festival that takes place there. The Umayyad Mosque in Damascus has within it

Women at the tomb of the fifteenth-century Sufi master Hacı Bayram Veli, Ankara, Turkey.

the tomb of John the Baptist, and the Umayyad Mosque in Aleppo has the tomb of John's father, Zechariah. These men are mentioned in the Qur'an, but many less-known people have been honored in this way as well, though on a much humbler scale. Examples include the Mamluk-period tomb of a *wali* named Sheikh Ramadan along a road in Galilee. Sufi master al-Junayd's tomb still stands today in Baghdad and, more than a thousand years since his death, is still visited by many. Rumi's tomb in Konya is a significant pilgrimage site and attracts thousands each year. At the buildings that housed his Sufi order, his large tomb is the centerpiece of the devotion of visitors. They utter prayers in front of his tomb and ask Allah's blessings upon him and them. As we have seen, pilgrimages to the tombs of the Shia imams and their family members are on a massive scale and are a major component of Shia worship.

Some birthplaces are venerated as well, including that of Abraham in Şanlıurfa, Turkey, with its complex that includes the cave of Abraham's birth, a spring, a park, a mosque, and other structures.

Religious Objects and Relics

Popular piety also places value in amulets to ward off evil forces, such as the "Hand of Fatima" amulet and the blue beads seen frequently in Turkey and elsewhere that provide protection from the Evil Eye. These are sometimes pinned on a baby's clothing for protection or hung in cars and trucks. Among the treasures of the Ottoman

The *basmala* in beautiful calligraphy, painted in "ebru," a traditional Turkish watercolor technique, Istanbul, Turkey.

sultans in Istanbul are hairs from Muhammad's beard and relics of other great people of the past, including Joseph's turban and Moses's staff. The spiritual reminders mentioned at the beginning of this chapter, including pictures and wall hangings, are also seen by some as having protective power. Muslims also find protection in the last two *suras* of the Qur'an, both of which are prayers that include the phrase, "I seek refuge."

Muslims do not worship objects, the prophets, or saints. Relics and activities of veneration—if they do not cross the line into forbidden areas—are a means by which ordinary people obtain *taqwa*, God consciousness.

Chapter 11

Private Life

Each chapter of this book could begin with a reminder that there are varieties of interpretations and applications of almost every topic pertaining to Islam. This may be particularly important in the following survey of private and family behavior. Muslims in different parts of the world had their own traditions when they converted, and some of those have become part of the broad Islamic culture in the minds of many people. Some customs have become closely identified with Islam, even though they may have no basis in the Qur'an and the *hadith*. In this chapter we will examine a variety of behaviors in which it is not always clear, even to Muslims themselves, what is Islamic and what is actually custom and tradition. The billion and a half people who identify themselves as Muslims are found in virtually every nation of the world, and they belong to hundreds of distinct ethnic groups. They live in nations with every known type of government. Some live in Muslim-majority environments, and some live where few other Muslims are found. In addition,

in all of those settings there are differences in how Islam is observed based on local adaptation, education, ancestral tradition, and perspective. Islam, as a result, has an amazing number of varieties.

This chapter will be somewhat personal and conversational, because much of the discussion will be based on behaviors that I have observed or have learned from Muslims I have known.

Finding a Husband or a Wife

Islam is clear in its teaching that there are to be no sexual relations outside of a marriage between a man and a woman. That principle governs all of the behaviors that precede marriage, including how one understands courtship and dating. The culture in many Islamic environments is that public displays of affection are usually inappropriate, and this is especially so among unmarried couples. So dating, to the extent that it exists, is often unlike what is found in some non-Muslim societies.

The traditional view is that parents have much greater wisdom and experience than their children, and thus it is the parents' responsibility to select spouses for them, or at least to guide them in that selection. But how the parental guidance is applied has a wide variety of manifestations. Not too many generations ago, virtually all Muslim marriages were arranged, but that is changing in many instances. Following are three examples from people I have known that show their experiences with this issue. I have changed their names for this narration.

I had friends from South Asia whose marriage was arranged when they were children. They were not hesitant to talk about their experience. They had known their whole lives that they were engaged but hardly knew each other until their wedding. They said that Westerners are accustomed to falling in love and then getting married, but in their culture they simply did it the other way around. They were thankful to their parents for making wise choices in their behalf, and they gave every impression of being a happy couple.

Maha and Ibrahim came to America from the same Muslim country to seek higher education. Both received degrees in the United States, and while they lived there, they met and fell in love. When Maha contacted her parents back at home and told them she was going to be married, her father was especially hurt. One of his most important duties as her father was to care for her, make a wise choice in her behalf for her marriage, and then turn her over to the care of her new husband. He felt that Maha, now very Americanized, had taken a track in life that devalued him and caused him to feel that he had failed in an important paternal responsibility. Although he remained very traditional to the end of his life, he came to accept the new reality.

Early in the twentieth century, the Aziz family moved to America from their Middle Eastern village. Traveling in the United States, they found a place where they wanted to settle down and raise a family, even though there were no other Muslims within hundreds of miles. Their son Musa was born there several years later and grew up as an American young man. When he was eighteen, his father took him back to his home village and arranged a marriage for him with a local young woman. After agonizing over the matter for a long time, Musa finally realized that he could not go through with the marriage, so he went back to the United States. The reaction in the village was mixed. Half of the people, he later recalled, were furious at him for dishonoring his parents, his relatives, and his fiancée. But the other half, he said, were proud of him for escaping from the undesirable situation.

I have taught Muslim students from the Middle East and South Asia who attended college in the United States. I would ask them, "Did your grandparents have arranged marriages?" The answer was almost always yes. "Did your parents have an arranged marriage?" Some answered yes, but in most cases the answer was no. Those of the parents' generation who did not have arranged marriages often underwent difficult experiences with their own parents as they pushed against custom to make their own marriage choices. Then I asked, "Are *you* going to have an arranged marriage?" The answer was, with one exception, emphatically no. The one exception was a young man from a very traditional home in Pakistan. He was comfortable with his situation and apparently with the choice as well.

A newlywed couple in Istanbul, Turkey, the bride wearing a *hijab* wedding dress.

This survey has obvious limitations, because the sample was made up entirely of Muslims who were more educated and more Westernized than most others. Even so, it is obvious that there is generational movement in attitudes on the topic of mate selection. With that in mind, no one should be surprised to learn that in the modern world, there are now Muslim-oriented internet dating sites that are becoming increasingly popular.

Males, Females, and Family

For most Muslims, religious principles play an important role in defining the nature of private and public life. This explains the norms that influence the clothing they wear, as we will see, and it also explains other aspects of the relationship between women and men.

Muslims are quick to mention that when Islam was first revealed, it was a step forward for Arabian women. The Qur'an denounces the custom of killing unwanted daughters, for example. Some historians, however, believe that early Islam created patterns of male dominance that continued for centuries. The Qur'an stipulates that a woman's inheritance is less than a man's, and the testimony of two women equals that of one man. Sharia law includes other provisions that assign different obligations and benefits to each. Some historians have pointed out that these laws reflect the realities of the early years of Islam, in which the burden of earning a living and providing for a family rested solely on the man, thus necessitating that society be ordered in this way.

In fact, the dominance of males is something that is very ancient and has been reflected in the majority of cultures around the world. In this, early Muslims shared similarities with their Christian, Zoroastrian, and pagan neighbors. Many religions have assumed different societal and domestic duties for men and women, and Islam is no different. The modern world has brought new perspectives to Muslims as it has for others, but even many progressive Muslims believe that Allah has decreed some roles to women and some different ones to men.

As in any culture, Islam shows a variety of family types, and the ideal is not always the norm. Marriage is expected for all who are of sound

mind, and it is valued strongly. How the roles of husband and wife are understood varies between cultures and between individual families, but in general Muslim marriages today resemble local patterns of the broader society more than those of Islam's early years. One scholar discusses the complementary roles of wives and husbands in this way:

> A common Islamic view of marriage is that a husband and wife need each other in order to be complete and fulfilled. The division of labor needed to maintain a household normally means that the husband works outside the home in the public sector, earning a livelihood for himself, his wife, and their children, and the wife concentrates her energies and talents in managing the family's domestic affairs. . . . Thoughtful and observant Muslims and others are both aware of and sensitive to the issues of injustice and subjugation, whether of women, children, or men; but they are also bent on preserving a traditional family structure because they believe that it is the most stable and honorable form for intimate social relations and the inculcation of ethical values, religious principles, and the formation of mature character. (F. M. Denny, *Introduction to Islam*, 4th ed., 276)

Many Muslim women are in the workforce, and Muslim families juggle economic and cultural concerns to best meet family needs, just as other families do. My friend Maha, introduced in the account above, explained how authority works in her marriage with Ibrahim. Although she is a highly educated woman who has had a professional career, in public Ibrahim typically does the talking. Within their home, however, she rules. Ibrahim did not disagree.

In the public sphere, Muslim women, like women elsewhere, are becoming more visible than in the generations of their mothers and grandmothers. Bangladesh, Indonesia, Kyrgyzstan, Pakistan, and Turkey—all of which are Muslim-majority countries—have already had women as presidents or prime ministers.

While Islam places sexual relations strictly within the sole confines of marriage, its attitude toward sex is positive, both as a means of bringing children into the world and as a means of finding fulfillment in marriage. Sex is to be enjoyed as a happy part of married life.

Polygamy (more precisely, polygyny, or marriage of a man to more than one woman) is allowed in Islam. The Qur'an teaches that a man may have up to four wives if he can treat them all equally (4.3). Yet the same *sura* concedes, "You will never be able to treat your wives with equal fairness, however much you may desire to do so" (4.129). Polygamy is legal in about one-fourth of the countries of the world, most of which have large Muslim populations. In some countries, such as India and the Philippines, it is legal for Muslims but not for anyone else. Polygamy has been part of Islamic reality since Muhammad's time, but today in many countries where it is legal it is also unaffordable, impractical, socially undesirable, and uncommon. Thus the vast majority of Muslims believe that it is untenable and therefore do not practice it. None of the Muslim students I mentioned above answered in the affirmative when I asked if they knew a polygamist. When I told them I had met polygamists, they were surprised. The ones I met were in a Bedouin encampment in the Sinai desert of Egypt, a culture that is very different from the environments from which those students came.

Divorce is permitted in Islam, but Muhammad reportedly said, "The most hated of permissible things to Allah is divorce." Islam has rules that govern divorce, and observant Muslims who wish to terminate a marriage must follow Sharia for the divorce to be valid within the context of Islam. The process favors the husband, for whom it is much easier than for the wife. Because many countries treat divorce as a civil matter, Muslims in many parts of the world need also to undergo civil proceedings to divorce according to the laws of the state.

Non-Muslims who visit some Muslim countries may notice very large homes in neighborhoods that do not look particularly affluent. Many of those are homes of extended families. It is not uncommon for extended and multigenerational families to live together under one roof. Islamic culture stresses the need to care for aged parents, and some observers have noted that Muslims generally do that better than many other people. In addition, family members with better economic resources are often found taking care of sibling families that are not as well off. I stayed with a Muslim family for three days in which the oldest brother (I will call him Jamal) was the primary breadwinner for several families. In his large home, which looked like a small apartment building, he housed his widowed mother, a sister and her husband and children, a brother and his wife and children, and an unmarried youngest brother. Jamal had a good job and provided most of the support for all of those families. I noticed, as a result, that his siblings were always very deferential to him and treated him with strict respect and obedience. At mealtimes or when Jamal wanted to provide drinks for his guests, the youngest brother came whenever he called and acted the part of a servant.

Islamic Names

When babies are born, parents often select names of important Muslims of the past or names that represent Islamic virtues. Thus many Muslim men bear the names of prophets or of other saintly or famous people from history. Names like Khadija, Fatima, and Aisha are still in use, as are Umar and Ali. The name Muhammad (and its variants, like Mehmet in Turkey) is the most common boy's name, and some Muslims follow the custom of having at least one male in the extended family with that name. Often baby girls and boys are named after relatives. Many men have names that contain the element *abd*, "servant of," followed by one of God's names. Examples include *Abdullah*, "Servant of Allah," and *Abdul-Jabbar*, "Servant of the Almighty." Sometimes people are given honorific names when they are adults by which they are commonly known thereafter. A Syrian friend always called me *Abu-Jonny*, "Father of Jonny," with reference to my firstborn son. "Father of" and "Mother of" are common elements in how many people are addressed, and some are known almost exclusively by those names.

In modern days, Muslims frequently do what other couples do when looking for a name for a newborn child—they turn to the internet, where several sites provide lists of possible Islamic names for both boys and girls.

Circumcision

Circumcision of males is a custom that is not original to Islam but was common in the Near East long before Muhammad's time. It involves cutting off the loose skin at the tip of the male organ. In Old Testament religion and then in Judaism, circumcision was a sign that the boy had entered into the covenant between God and his people. Many Muslims understand it in much the same way. Abraham, according to a *hadith*, circumcised himself at Allah's command (Bukhari 6298), thus setting a pattern to be followed by others. Despite not being mentioned in the Qur'an, circumcision has been a Muslim practice since the beginning, and it spread with Islam as Islam moved into other regions. Islamic legal experts have been divided as to whether it is obligatory or only recommended. In either case, it is very widespread today. The only commonly accepted age requirement is that it is done before puberty, and in many cultures there is no specific ritual attached to it and it takes place in a medical facility. In Turkey and in some other areas, there is considerable fanfare and celebration attached to circumcision as a coming-of-age ritual. Turkish boys, usually between seven and eleven years old, dress up in royal attire and are sometimes accompanied to or from the procedure with parades and family celebrations.

What is sometimes called circumcision of females is a custom that likewise existed independently of Islam and then became part of it in the eyes of many. Widely criticized by healthcare professionals and Muslim and non-Muslim human-rights activists as "female genital mutilation" (or sometimes "female genital cutting"), the practice involves the cutting off of parts of a girl's external sex organs. Found primarily in Indonesia, Egypt, and Sub-Saharan Africa, most who practice it are Muslims who do it because they believe it is Islamic, even though it is a custom that developed elsewhere and is not found in the Qur'an. The practice is also found among other populations in those areas, including among some African Christians. There are different varieties of the practice, some being more intrusive than others. Proponents believe that some form of cutting, usually to remove or reduce the size of the clitoris, is necessary to lesson female sexual desire and thus promote chastity. Muslim Sharia scholars have

had differing views, but most of them now speak out against the practice as un-Islamic.

Clothing

The distinction between public and private spheres in Islam is no more apparent than in women's clothing. *Hijab* is the term used for a woman's clothing that covers her in accordance with Islamic teachings. The word is used for the concept of covering in general, or it can be used synonymously with "headscarf," which is the most recognized manifestation of *hijab*. The issue is public modesty. At the most private level in a Muslim's life, certain intimacies are appropriate, and familiarity and openness with close family members are desirable. *Hijab* exists to assure that those familiarities that are allowable in private are not shared outside of that private setting.

Within the home, an observant Muslim woman wears whatever she wants, so long as she is alone or interacting with close family members. Her home in the company of her family members is protective space. When she leaves and goes into the community, *hijab* allows her to take that protective space with her as she moves about, and it has allowed millions of Muslim women to work, shop, and travel conveniently. *Hijab* provides psychological boundaries for her and for the people she encounters that remind all of them that she is a Muslim woman, and her space is not to be violated. But unfortunately, it does not always protect women from harassment.

Once while I was in Syria, I was eating with friends near the door of a restaurant that was immediately next to a lingerie shop. Women dressed from head to toe in flowing black were at the shop window examining and discussing the colorful items of intimate apparel that were on display there. My non-Muslim friend was taken aback that women so modestly dressed would wear such things. *Hijab*, however, is not about the private habits of Muslim women but about how they choose to present themselves in public space. The "rules" vary from culture to culture, region to region, and within cultures and families. Some women cover all but their hands, feet, and faces, while some even cover the face except for a space for the eyes. Some wear Western clothing and a

Headscarves in some areas are fairly uniform, as in Mit-Rahineh, Egypt (above). Elsewhere, as in Istanbul, Turkey (below), they can be varied and colorful.

headscarf, but some observant Muslim women choose not to wear any form of *hijab*.

The use of *hijab* is more common now than it was only a few decades ago. Part of that comes from the fact that more women are at universities and in the workforce and thus need to move about in society. But part of it comes from the fact that many women see *hijab* as a means of publicly identifying themselves as Muslims. There are other reasons as well: many women have said that they wear *hijab* so they don't have to fix their hair when they go out, and for some women *hijab* is even a fashion statement.

The Qur'an and the *hadith* have actually very little to say about this topic, and the references in the Qur'an are addressed to Muhammad's wives and not to Muslim women in general. While many Sharia experts have ruled that *hijab* is required for an observant woman, some endorse the practice but say it is not required.

Shaking Hands

There is no explicit law in Islam about unrelated women and men shaking hands, and opinions of the custom vary. Some women prefer not to shake hands with men, but often it is men who are reticent to shake hands with women.

Food

Like many other religions, Islam has rules regarding what one may eat and drink. The Qur'an identifies as *haram* (forbidden) the consumption of alcohol, animals that die on their own, pork, and any meat that was sacrificed to a god other than Allah (2.173). Muslim scholars teach that drugs and other addictive substances are also prohibited, and some Muslims also avoid smoking for this reason. For practical application today, the prohibitions of pork and alcohol are the most recognizable.

Once in Syria with three other non-Muslims and a Syrian friend, we had a visit with a local police captain. Knowing that we were not Muslims, he asked if we ate pork. He was repelled at our answer. Muslims do not eat pork not only because it is prohibited by their religion but also because most Muslims view pigs as disgusting animals and therefore foul creatures to eat. When our host offered

me a cigarette, I told him I didn't smoke because my religion discourages it. He responded, "What kind of religion is this that lets you eat pork but doesn't let you smoke!?"

Hospitality

The Qur'an instructs believers to care for strangers and travelers, and I have personally witnessed Muslims being faithful to this command. On one occasion in Gaza, a non-Muslim friend and I were invited to several dinners in the homes of different families. Our hosts were men, as were the others who had been invited to the meals. The wives of our hosts prepared the meals in their kitchens and usually did not come out even to greet us. When they did, however, they had their heads covered because even though they were in their own homes, our presence there changed what they felt was appropriate to wear.

I once was with an American friend in a rental car driving in Jordan. We had a flat tire on a desert road. There was a spare tire in the trunk, but it was flat. We jacked up the car, took the tire off, and stood by the side of the road to hitch a ride into town. The first vehicle that we saw was a small local bus, and we and our tire were invited in. The people in the bus discussed our need, and the driver took us to a tire shop in town and would not let us pay for the ride. Our tire was repaired, and the man who fixed it wouldn't let us pay him either. With our repaired tire, we stood out on the road again, and the first car that arrived picked us up and took us back to our car. We were soon on our way. We did not get the spare fixed because we were in a hurry.

The next morning as we were driving, we got another flat tire. Again we jacked up the car and stood by the side of the road. The first car that arrived took us to a tire shop in the next town, and we got the tire fixed. We stood by the side of the road again, and again the first car that came by took us in and took us to our car.

Hospitality is a virtue that Muslims take very seriously. Once in Syria my friends and I were driving south when we flagged down a car driving north to ask the driver for directions. We learned that we were on the right road, so we continued on our way. Several kilometers later, we noticed that the driver from whom we had asked directions was now driving behind us, honking to get our attention and trying to pull us over. When we stopped, he expressed his embarrassment and apologies that he had not invited us to his home for tea. We were on a tight schedule and could not accept his invitation, but his kindness reminded us that we were among Muslim friends who heeded the Qur'an's call for hospitality to strangers.

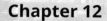

Chapter 12

Islamism and Jihad

Terms and Names to Know

fundamentalism, Islamism, Islamist, jihad, lesser jihad, greater jihad, Hezbollah, terrorism

Islam, like all other religions with ancient origins, exists in a world today that is not the same as the one from which it came. Although Muslims believe that the Qur'an is eternal, the world it describes is very different from the one in which most Muslims find themselves now. The question for any religion that wants to survive is, "How do we take the founding documents and traditions and make them work for the circumstances of the modern world?"

The word *fundamentalism* first found widespread usage with reference to conservative Protestant Christians in America. It is frequently used in discussions of Islam—almost always without being understood clearly. Fundamentalism in general is a response to changes in the world that one perceives as threatening. If we take conservative Christians as an example, criticism of the Bible and other modern ideas convinced many of them that society was going in the wrong direction. When that happens, a natural instinct that many experience is to retrench, retreat to the

fundamentals, and fight to preserve the world they once knew.

Muslims are not immune from this instinct, and all over the world they are facing challenges that arise as the societies in which they live continue to be exposed to outside influences. In matters of religious importance, the fundamentalist instinct is an especially sensitive matter. How should believers react to modern society when they are convinced that their religion is divine and yet the world is opposing it?

Islamism

Islam guides personal behavior and directs Muslims in many aspects of their lives, from the sacred and ceremonial to the seemingly mundane. The word *Islamism* is used to describe the effort to take the religion and make it dominant in the political sphere, that is, to have the laws of Islam govern not only private life but public life as well. Islamists are those who argue that because their religion is from God, it should govern society just as it governs private behavior. Whereas *Islamic* is a religious term, *Islamist* is a political term that implies religious justification for political claims.

The New Testament was written with the idea that believers in Jesus would live in a non-Christian world ruled by others. The Qur'an is very different. Although the early *suras* show a small religious group persecuted by surrounding forces, the later *suras* from Medina reveal a society in which Islam was the government. Religious leadership and community leadership were the same. Early Muslims and many Muslims today consider this to be the ideal. Yet millions live in countries where secular laws prevail, and millions of others live in Muslim-majority countries that are not sufficiently Islamic in their eyes. The instinct for some in these situations is to long for a world governed by the Sharia and to wonder how that world can be brought about. Questions include "What would such a government look like?" and "How—or to what extent—would Sharia be instituted in it?"

When asked about instituting specific laws that are often identified as part of Sharia, such as the ownership of slaves, whipping fornicators a hundred times, or cutting off the hands of criminals, many modern Muslims would prefer to leave those in the past. This highlights why establishing Sharia as the law of the land is a difficult topic in the modern world. Muslims, like adherents of any religion, have those among them who are very socially conservative and those who are more socially liberal. There are those who feel that the laws that governed the *umma* in the seventh century should still be applied the same way today, and there are those who say that those laws need to be adapted or reinterpreted to meet the realities of modern society. There are many variants in between. The key, perhaps, is to identify fundamental Islamic principles (rather than specific applications) as the embodiment of Sharia and to apply those in law. This in fact is what a majority of Muslims want when they express a desire for Sharia in modern legal systems. It is not much different from what some Christians want when they argue for "biblical principles" to be applied in law.

In actual practice, most Muslim-majority nations have systems in place in which some application of Sharia governs such things as marriage, divorce, and inheritance, while civil courts deal with criminal matters. Thus in those countries, the strong Qur'anic criminal punishments are not applied.

How would a Sharia-based government be organized? The most conservative Muslims reject the idea of democracy and forbid their followers from even voting in elections. They argue that to participate in a democratic system is to acknowledge that humans, in place of God, have a right to rule and create laws. But this is the opinion of only a minority. The majority of Muslims, not only in Europe and North America but also in the Islamic homelands, say they favor a democratic system of government, though one in which Islamic principles are still followed. In saying so, they are expressing the position that democracy is not merely permissible but that it is consistent with Islam, or even required by it. The consensus of believers, as we have seen, is a major cornerstone of Islamic legal philosophy, and God commands in the Qur'an that believers "conduct their affairs by mutual consultation" (42.38). For some, these are strong arguments for democracy, as is the idea that the *umma* will never agree on an error. God's unique sovereignty suggests that putting power into the hands of dictators violates divine will. Muslims who live in functioning democracies generally recognize that under their democratic systems they have greater peace and greater opportunities to live their religion than they would under other systems of government, and thus they participate in elections and in other secular civic engagements.

Jihad

The word *jihad* means "striving," "effort," or "exertion." Muslim scholars typically use it in two ways, identifying a "lesser jihad" and a "greater jihad."

The lesser jihad is fighting to defend Islam in the context of armed conflict. The Qur'an and the *hadith* literature both justify war against those who fight against Islam. The consensus view is that it must be undertaken by the state and not by individuals, it must be defensive, and civilians must not be targeted. Most Muslims today view the lesser jihad in those terms.

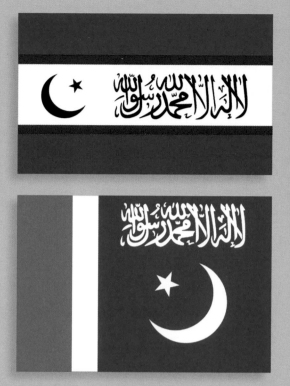

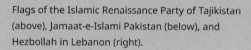

Flags of the Islamic Renaissance Party of Tajikistan (above), Jamaat-e-Islami Pakistan (below), and Hezbollah in Lebanon (right).

The Islamic Renaissance Party and Jamaat-e-Islami Pakistan are examples of Sunni Islamist organizations dedicated to creating Sharia-based Islamic states through participation in elections. Both had mixed success over the years. Hezbollah, a Shia organization, is one of the world's most successful Islamist groups. It functions as a recognized political party in Lebanon's multireligious society, but it also has a significant army and has powerful influence over much of Lebanon's territory.

The greater jihad is the more important of the two and represents how most Muslims choose to understand the word. It is an effort in which all believers are engaged all the time. This is the struggle against self that Muslims undertake to keep firmly on the path of Islam. It is a struggle against one's weaknesses and lack of self-control, a struggle to overcome natural inclinations and temptations, and a struggle to live a life in which one is ever conscious of Allah.

Terrorism is a phenomenon that exists independently of anything Islamic and has been used by many people for a variety of causes. We can define it as the use of violence to make political statements with the goal of changing the behavior of others through fear. Terrorism is "hate crime" on a grand scale. As such, it is more message than warfare, but if the message is delivered loudly enough, it becomes a very effective weapon to influence the behavior of others. Terrorists do not see themselves as murderers but as soldiers, which enables them to justify their actions. Even if they kill noncombatants, those deaths are justifiable to them either because the victims were part of the system and are therefore guilty themselves or simply because their deaths serve a greater good. When terrorism is mentioned, Westerners often think of bombings in Europe or of the September 11, 2001, attacks on the United States. Yet most victims of terror perpetrated by Islamist extremists have been Muslims themselves, victims of fellow Muslims who are seeking increased power or legitimacy for their causes.

The vast majority of Muslims reject the idea of terrorism and are horrified to see their religion associated with it. They find the idea repugnant and are especially repelled by the notion of martyrdom associated with activities like suicide bombings, which they consider contrary to Islam. Most Muslims reject the notion that killing civilians can be justified in any way. Yet, as we will see in chapters 13 and 14, there are some strands of modern Islam that embrace political violence as a useful tool in Allah's service. And unfortunately, those extremists have persuaded many non-Muslims that they represent what Islam is really about.

Chapter 13

Modern Political Challenges

Part 1 (Egypt, Palestine, Saudia Arabia, Iran, and Afghanistan)

Terms and Names to Know

Muslim Brotherhood, al-Banna, colonialism, Qutb, Nasser, Sadat, al-Jihad, Mubarak, Arab Spring, Hamas, Wahhabism, ibn Saud, Mossadegh, Mohammad Reza Shah, Khomeini, Islamic Republic of Iran, Khamenei, Khatami, Taliban, bin Laden, al-Qaeda, al-Zawahiri

This chapter and chapter 14 present surveys of modern religion-based political challenges in Muslim-majority countries and look at how those countries have responded to the challenges. What follows will not be about the Islamic world in general but will be a look at only a few selected countries that appear often in news reports. My goal is to enable readers to understand what is going on in these countries when they watch or read the news. I will provide only an outline of the topics, and the discussion will not attempt to be up-to-date but will simply introduce the historical developments and issues that have led those countries to where they are today. Needless to say, each of these situations is a work in progress. In this chapter we will look at countries in the Middle East, and readers will notice how developments in one country often have an impact on others.

Egypt

The Muslim Brotherhood was established in Egypt in 1928 by Hasan al-Banna (1906–49). It developed into an organization that served several needs, functioning as a political action organization, labor union, cultural-educational society, and social club. On the large scale, Banna's effort, followed by his successors in the Brotherhood, was to reject Western influences in the Islamic world and to replace secular governments with Islamic-oriented governments under Sharia law. After the Brotherhood's founding in Egypt, it spread to surrounding Arab countries.

The Brotherhood, and other groups like it, grew up in a period in which most of the Muslim-majority nations in the world were under the control of European colonial powers, particularly the

Hasan al-Banna, founder of the Muslim Brotherhood.

Netherlands in Indonesia, Britain in India and in much of the Middle East, and France in Syria and in parts of Africa. Modernists and reformers realized that the West had much to offer in many areas, but they struggled with how to retain a distinctive Islamic identity while accommodating a changing world. Most agreed that colonialism was an affront not only to the subjugated peoples but also to Islam. The United States had no colonies in Muslim lands, so Americans were initially viewed more favorably than Europeans. America's image was tarnished as time progressed, as Banna and others became increasingly aware of widespread racism in the United States, its support for Jewish immigrants in Palestine at the expense of the Arab population, and as America became most closely identified with Western culture in general.

One of Banna's ideological successors in the Brotherhood was Sayyid Qutb (1906–66), an Egyptian writer and educator who was one of the most important Islamist thinkers of his time.

A prolific author, he influenced generations of Islamists and still remains an important voice in Islamist thought. He lived in the United States during 1948–50 on an assignment to research American education. Already hostile to the West, his experience confirmed his beliefs about the United States. He disliked profoundly what he saw, and he characterized America as a place of crude music, immodest women, crass materialism, and an absence of moral character. The contrast between America and his idealized view of Islamic culture fed his revolutionary ideas, which included not only disdain for the West but also contempt for non-Islamic Arab governments.

Qutb believed that there was a great conflict going on between Allah's true religion and the laws and cultures of corrupt humans; no compromise or reconciliation could be made between them. In the mid-1960s while he was in an Egyptian prison, he wrote his most important book, *Milestones*, which was a call for an Islamist reinvention of the world. He denounced "any system in which the final decisions are referred to human beings, and in which the sources of all authority are human." All authority needed to be returned to Allah, and the "usurpers," that is, secular rulers, needed to be "thrown out." In their place and in place of all human laws, Allah's laws must be enforced, and "the final decision in all affairs be according to these laws." He called for nothing less than "the establishing of the dominion of God on earth, the abolishing of the dominion of man, the taking away of sovereignty from the usurper to revert it to God, and the bringing about of the enforcement of the Divine Law (Shariah)." He predicted that because those who held earthly rule "are not going to give up their power merely through preaching," other means would be required and justified to take power from them. Qutb argued that this quest was not only to liberate Muslims from their bondage to human laws but to bring the entire world under the dominion of Allah. In this effort, he downplayed the notion of the greater jihad and strongly criticized Muslim scholars who argued that jihad was only to be understood as an act of self-defense. He gave as positive examples Abu-Bakr, Umar, and Uthman, who used military conquest as a means of spreading Islam (*Milestones*, chapter 4).

Sayyid Qutb in prison before being executed in 1966.

The secular Egyptian government took all of this personally and considered Qutb to be a threat. President Gamal Abdel Nasser suppressed the Brotherhood during the 1950s and 1960s and imprisoned Qutb for his revolutionary ideas. In 1966 Nasser had Qutb executed. Nasser's successor, Anwar Sadat, continued the official suppression in the 1970s, but not as aggressively.

Another Egyptian Islamist group, al-Jihad, had a more militant agenda. In 1981 members of that group murdered President Sadat. The group continued its terrorist activities in the following decades, including the 1997 massacre of sixty-two tourists (mostly Swiss and Japanese). During the administration of Sadat's successor, Hosni Mubarak, the government had an uneasy truce with the Brotherhood. Al-Jihad continued its terrorism, however, with the goal of destroying Egypt's economy and thereby causing the fall of the government, which would open the door for an Islamic state.

In December 2010, a Tunisian street vendor set himself on fire to protest how he was treated by his government. That set off a chain of anti-government protests in Tunisia and then in other countries in which people went to the streets to demand change. The movement, seen as a hopeful sign of rebellion against oppressive rulers, soon earned the name "Arab Spring." Tunisia's government was overthrown in mid-January 2011, and within a month the Mubarak government in Egypt was overthrown as well.

Following free elections, the Muslim Brotherhood, now sponsoring its own political party, came to power in Egypt, an event that was heralded as a great Islamist victory achieved through voting. The new government faced significant challenges both from the military and from citizens concerned about its policies. Subsequent mass protests revealed a strong popular concern among many Egyptians that an Islamist government was not what they wanted. In 2013 the military overthrew the government and took control of the country. Despite its being one of the largest political groups in Egypt, the Muslim Brotherhood was outlawed, and massive waves of arrests of Brotherhood members followed.

Palestine

The situation in Palestine deserves a brief mention in this chapter, because it is common to hear that the conflict between the Palestinians and the Israelis is a religious struggle between Judaism and Islam that has been going on for centuries, perhaps since the days of Isaac and Ishmael. This is not true. It is a political conflict over possession of land. Two peoples, the Israelis and the Palestinians, both lay claim to the same small area as their national homeland. Both have had a presence there for centuries, both provide historical arguments for their presence in the land, and each side seeks to live there in peace and security. For the most part, the conflict began in the 1880s when Jews began migrating to Palestine in increasing numbers to escape anti-Jewish violence and then extermination attempts by Europeans. The Arab population, fearing the loss of its land to the new immigrants, resisted.

Islamists and ordinary Muslims since the generation of Hasan al-Banna viewed the influx of European Jews as continuing colonialism, and they sided with their fellow Arabs who lost political power when the State of Israel was established in 1948. The support of the United States for the Jewish state led many to describe the Americans and the Israelis as new Crusaders, intent on exerting control in Muslim lands.

In the 1990s and early 2000s, a Palestinian Islamist group called Hamas became increasingly influential. A distant offshoot of Egypt's Muslim Brotherhood, its goal was to liberate Palestine from the Israelis and create there an Islamic state. Supported by money from other countries, Hamas built clinics and schools and provided humanitarian aid and social services for Palestinians, many of whom were refugees from their homes in what is now Israel. Hamas's activities brought it into conflict with the secular Palestine Liberation Organization and Palestine's civil administration, the Palestinian National Authority. Thus ensued a clash between secular and Islamist political visions for Palestine's future. Hamas won the Palestinian elections in 2006 but was forced out of power by combined Israeli and American pressure. Rivalry between the Palestinian groups turned into a military conflict in 2007, and Hamas took control of Gaza and became its acting government, bringing a considerable portion of Palestine's population under an Islamist administration.

Although Hamas and its supporters wrapped the Arab-Israeli conflict in the mantle of Islam, not all Palestinian Muslims favored the idea of being governed by Islamists.

Saudi Arabia

Modern Saudi Arabia is the result of a marriage between three entities—Wahhabi Islam, the Al Saud family, and oil.

Muhammad al-Wahhab was an Islamic preacher who lived in Arabia in the eighteenth century. He believed that Islam had been corrupted by worldly forces, and he set out to reform it to comply with his very strict interpretation of Sharia law. The movement he started, commonly called Wahhabism, is often described as "puritanical" Islam, and indeed it is. He had very strong feelings about innovations to Islam that, in his opinion, took it off its divine course, and he advocated strict enforcement of what he considered the purest form of the religion. Most notable was his campaign to obliterate the tombs and shrines of *walis* to which people made pilgrimages, which he considered *shirk*—idol worship or polytheism.

Al-Wahhab made an alliance with the ruler of a local tribe, Muhammad ibn Saud. Ibn Saud would support and promote al-Wahhab's version of Islam, and al-Wahhab would then support and give legitimacy to ibn Saud's claim to rule. The alliance has continued to the present day. In the

early decades of the 1900s, Abd al-Aziz ibn Saud did what his ancestors had been unable to do and united almost all of the Arabian Peninsula under his control with him as king. Thus the kingdom of Saudi Arabia was born, becoming an independent country in 1932. Over the years, he was followed as king by several of his sons, and the kingdom now continues under a new generation. Ibn Saud's descendants now number in the thousands, and they are the privileged upper class in what is one of the most unique societies in the world.

Oil was discovered in Arabia in the 1930s, and in a very short time its importance was realized. By then the industrial world's demand for it was exploding, and the enormous reserves in Saudi territory were discovered just in time to meet growing needs. This was a recipe for unimaginable amounts of money to flow to the royal family, and indeed they and their government have become extraordinarily wealthy from the extraction and sale of the precious commodity.

As the Saudis grew in wealth and influence, so also did Wahhabi Islam, the religious arm of the Saudi state. Saudi Arabia has one of the strictest applications of Islamic law in the world, with rules that Muslims in many other countries find hard to imagine. As examples, Saudi women were not

King Abd al-Aziz ibn Saud of Saudi Arabia (left) conferring with US president Franklin D. Roosevelt on an American naval ship in 1945.

allowed to drive cars until 2018, and the kingdom holds public beheadings of criminals. With all the wealth available, the Saudi religious establishment has undertaken efforts to export its brand of Islam to other countries. The Saudis have built mosques all over the world as well as theological schools to teach Muslims the Wahhabi way. Saudi Arabia wants to be seen as the standard-bearer for all of Sunni Islam.

The huge oil reserves under Arabian sand have made the close association between Saudi Arabia and the United States perhaps inevitable. Observers of the two countries have said that one of the modern world's most striking paradoxes is that the United States, with its pluralistic society and democratic laws and traditions, should have a special relationship with what critics consider an intolerant political/religious system governed by an oppressive monarchy. As long as the United States depends on Saudi oil, however, that relationship will likely continue.

Iran

Iran's population is overwhelmingly Shia, and for centuries Iran has been the Shia counterbalance to the Sunni majority that is found in other countries.

In 1953 the United Kingdom and the United States helped to bring about the overthrow of Iran's democratically elected president, Mohammad Mossadegh, in order to place the power of the country firmly in the hands of its king, Mohammad Reza Shah. Their complaint against Mossadegh was that he and the democratically elected parliament had passed laws that enabled Iran to nationalize its oil resources, which previously had been under the control of the British. American and British intelligence agencies organized the coup, financed it, and induced politicians and military officials to make it happen.

Oil was discovered in Iran in 1908, but the Iranians had not profited from it to the extent that the Saudis had because early contracts with the British allowed the United Kingdom to control Iranian oil production and retain most of the revenue from it. In the 1950s a variety of forces combined, or competed, to make Iran what it was then—Shia Islam, oil, a desire for progress, and a

Mohammad Mossadegh, prime minister of Iran 1951–53.

longing for democracy. Uncertainties about Iran's future caused concerns for the Americans and the British. They feared that an independent-minded Iran might lean toward its massive neighbor to the north, the Soviet Union. The Shah, with all the power in his hands, would presumably give the Americans and the British a more compliant partner who would support their own geopolitical interests.

The Shah stayed in power until 1979, propped up mainly by the United States. For most of that time, he proved to be a dependable supplier of oil to the West. In geopolitics he played the Soviets and the Americans against each other rather successfully, yet for the most part the Americans found that he was useful. He did much to Westernize Iran, and foreign business interests were very successful there. But to his own people, the Shah was seen as increasingly oppressive and brutal, and neither Iran's democrats nor its Islamists wanted him to stay in power.

The Iranian revolution of 1979 was one of the most remarkable political events of the twentieth century. It was a popular uprising against the Shah powered by the will of the people, yet its unlikely political guides were the Shia clergy. The leader was Ayatollah Ruhollah Khomeini, who had earned his great status by his academic work and teaching. In his publications and lectures, Khomeini argued not only that the *ulama*'s position as experts in Islamic law made them the worthiest successors to the imams but also that governmental power should be vested in them rather than in secular leaders. Because of the revolutionary nature of Khomeini's ideas, the Shah expelled him from the country. Khomeini kept his message alive in Iran by having his lectures recorded and smuggled into the country, where they were widely copied and disseminated. As uprisings were taking place in Iran and the Shah's rule was starting to fall apart, revolutionaries flocked to Khomeini in his exile in hopes of bringing about his return to Iran. He became

the symbol of the revolution. When the Shah was forced to flee the country, Khomeini returned in triumph and ultimately defeated his rivals within the revolutionary movement. Iran's long history of monarchy was over, and a new era was to begin.

In the following months, Khomeini and his allies created the Islamic Republic of Iran, the modern world's first major theocracy. Its constitution gives great power to the *ulama*. The supreme leader, originally Khomeini himself, would be a Shia cleric who would have ultimate authority in the country. Beneath him would be a popularly elected president and a popularly elected parliament, as well as local governors elected by the people. The result was a hybrid system that

Ruhollah Khomeini (right), supreme leader of Iran, at the 1981 inauguration of Ali Khamenei (left) as the country's president. Khomeini, the chief architect of the 1979 Iranian Revolution, served as Iran's supreme leader from 1979 until his death in 1989. Khamenei was twice elected president, serving 1981–89. Following Khomeini's death, Khamenei was chosen to succeed him as supreme leader.

had significant democratic elements but which was ultimately under the control of the clergy. In order to run for election, one had to be approved by a body of clergy called the Guardian Council, who vetted candidates for their Islamic suitability and thus controlled who could run for elections.

Khomeini and his closest followers were intensely hostile to the United States, which they blamed for the overthrow of Mossadegh's government and for assisting the Shah in his oppressive rule. When rioters took over the US embassy in Tehran in 1979, the Iranian leaders turned a blind eye and for over a year did not return the hostages that were taken. The two countries severed all diplomatic relations.

Mohammed Khatami emerged as a political reformer who served as Iran's president from 1997 to 2005. His election was brought about as a result of widespread dissatisfaction with the Islamic government, and many of his supporters were women and young voters. He reached out to the West in ways that his predecessors had not, and he worked to liberalize the system that had been in place since the 1979 Revolution. It was during his tenure that the Sunni terrorists of al-Qaeda attacked the United States on September 11, 2001. President Khatami and Iran's Supreme Leader condemned the attacks publicly. The mayor of Tehran sent a message of sympathy to the mayor of New York, and Iranian sport fans held a moment of silence during a soccer match. In sympathy with those who had died in the attacks, candlelight vigils took place in Tehran.

Observers noted that those gestures of goodwill should have opened a new era in US-Iranian relations, but they did not. Only four months after the September 11 attacks, US president George W. Bush publicly called Iran part of an "axis of evil" that "exports terror" and seeks "to threaten the peace of the world." Khatami's reformist efforts were weakened by the statements, and ordinary Iranians felt a sense of betrayal. The Guardian Council, with its responsibility to assure the Islamic credentials of all candidates, became increasingly conservative and selective. They rejected most of Khatami's reformist allies in parliament when they came up for reelection, and thus the next parliament was much more religiously conservative and hostile to Khatami and his efforts. In the end, Khatami's reforms did not

accomplish much, and in the next presidential election he was replaced by an outspoken supporter of Islamist rule who was more inclined to work in line with the *ulama*. Tensions between reformers and conservatives continue.

Iran's Shia Islam, with its veneration of the tombs of the imams and their families, is directly antithetical to Saudi Arabia's Wahhabi Islam. Both the Saudis and the Iranians have used Sunni-Shia animosity in recent years to set themselves up as protectors of their respective brands of Islam. The rivalry between these two nations has fed into several continuing political problems in other countries as well. Notable among these is a long-lasting and devastating civil war in Yemen between the Sunnis and the Zaidi Shia, in which Saudi Arabia and Iran played major roles.

Afghanistan

Afghanistan was a puppet state of the Soviet Union in the 1970s. In 1979 when its government proved unable to administer the country to Moscow's satisfaction, the Soviets invaded and took control. In response, the Afghans rose up to fight against the invaders to drive them out. They were joined by Islamists from other countries who wanted to help in the jihad to liberate a Muslim country. The United States provided assistance to the jihadis, and in 1989, after a long and bloody insurgency, the Soviet army was forced to leave.

In the aftermath of the Soviet departure from Afghanistan, different groups vied for power. Eventually an Islamist organization called the Taliban gained control of much of the country. They were followers of a very strict version of Islam that was not unlike Wahhabism. For the most part, the West ignored the Taliban until they made the news by blowing up some huge ancient Buddha statues in 2001, earning them outrage from people around the world. While most observant Muslims have no problem preserving the monuments of the civilizations that preceded Islam, for the Taliban the statues represented idol worship and *shirk* and needed to be destroyed.

After leaving Afghanistan, many of the foreign jihadis who had fought there vowed to continue the struggle against other targets. Among them was a young Saudi millionaire, Usama bin Laden (1957–2011), who in time became the leader of a group called al-Qaeda. One of his chief assistants was Dr. Ayman al-Zawahiri, head of Egypt's al-Jihad organization. The jihadis of al-Qaeda waged war against those they considered enemies of Islam wherever they could strike against them, and soon the United States became a major target. In 1998 al-Qaeda bombed two US embassies in Africa, killing hundreds of African civilians. They struck at many targets and eventually moved back into Afghanistan, where the Taliban provided a safe haven for them.

On September 11, 2001, al-Qaeda conducted its most dramatic operation, a joint suicide attack on New York and Washington, DC. The response from the United States was to invade Afghanistan to destroy al-Qaeda and remove the Taliban. After many years of fighting, neither of those goals was reached, although the Taliban were forced to flee the capital. The US helped put in place a secular government, but the Taliban continued to fight against it as part of a broader civil war that went on for many years. Most of al-Qaeda's members were killed or driven out of Afghanistan, but some moved on to other locations to continue the fight against their enemies. Some of the fighters found a new home in Iraq in the chaos that was caused there when US forces removed the government of Saddam Hussein.

Usama bin Laden (left) with Dr. Ayman al-Zawahiri in 2001. Al-Zawahiri joined Egypt's Muslim Brotherhood as a teenager and later became a leader of al-Jihad. He was arrested and served time in prison following the murder of Egyptian president Anwar Sadat. He later made his way to Afghanistan, where he merged al-Jihad into bin Laden's organization, al-Qaeda. When bin Laden was killed by US forces in 2011, al-Zawahiri became al-Qaeda's leader.

Chapter 14

Modern Political Challenges

Part 2 (Iraq, Syria, Turkey, Nigeria, and Indonesia)

Terms and Names to Know

Saddam Hussein, Islamic State in Iraq and Syria (ISIS), al-Baghdadi, Assad, Alawites, Atatürk, Özal, Erdoğan, Boko Haram, Shekau, syncretism

In chapter 13 we looked at countries in the Middle East. This chapter continues the narrative in that area and shows how developments in Iraq and Syria have been influenced by those in other lands. We then will examine Turkey, which straddles secularism and Islamism just as it straddles Europe and Asia. Then we will look at recent religious developments in Nigeria in Africa, and in Indonesia in South Asia.

Iraq

Iraq's population is about 65 percent Shia and 30 percent Sunni, with the rest comprised of Christians and others. Most of Shiism's holiest places are in Iraq, including the tombs of Imam Ali in Najaf and Imam Husayn in Karbala, both of which have been destinations for throngs of Shia pilgrims since the seventh century.

Saddam Hussein, a secular Sunni Muslim, rose to power in 1979 and ruled Iraq as a military dictator until he was removed by force in 2003. His state was outwardly and inwardly secular, and he did not allow Islamic influence in government in any substantial way. He obtained and maintained his power with brutal efficiency. Because he was the Sunni ruler of a population that was mostly Shia, he knew that the power of Shia religious tradition would always be a potential threat to his control. He staffed his government and his military leadership overwhelmingly with Sunni supporters, and he sometimes imprisoned and executed Shia leaders. As a secular state that opposed Islamism in every way, Iraq was a very different place from its neighbor to the east, the Islamic Republic of Iran.

Guided by the idea that Iraq's population would welcome Saddam's elimination and embrace democracy, the United States sent forces into Iraq in 2003, removed Saddam from power, and destroyed his government and military. Iraq's Shia majority was suspicious of America's intentions

Saddam Hussein of Iraq sometimes used Islamic symbols if they served his political interests. One of his palaces featured nine-meter-high busts of him wearing helmets depicting the dome of the Dome of the Rock in Jerusalem. The helmets include the crescent moon on the top, a common Islamic symbol.

but welcomed the end of Saddam's rule. Instead of the smooth transition to democratic government that the United States anticipated, Iraq entered into a bloody period of chaos and civil war. A government was created and voting took place, but most of the Sunnis refused to take part. The Shia-led government proved to be ineffective, and the country became unmanageable. The absence of governmental control led to the ascendency of Iraq's Shia clergy and the extension of their influence into political matters. Ordinary Iraqi Shia felt loyalties to their religious leaders that they had never felt to their government, so some clergy soon developed the equivalent of states within the state, including armies.

Al-Qaeda's Usama bin Laden viewed Saddam Hussein as an enemy and called him an infidel, an apostate from Islam. When Saddam was removed, the Sunni jihadist group al-Qaeda in Iraq, which included remnants of bin Laden's fighters from Afghanistan, stepped into the vacuum. They began a vicious war against Iraq's Shia population. Their weapon was terror attacks, in large part against the mosques and tombs of the imams and against pilgrims who worshipped

there. Bin-Laden and many of the jihadis who followed his example were Wahhabis or adherents of similar Sunni movements, and they viewed the Shia as apostates and their veneration of tombs as *shirk*. Thus for them, pilgrimage sites and Shia worshippers, wherever they could be found, were fair targets for terror attacks.

After Iraq's western neighbor, Syria, descended into civil conflict in 2012, the Sunni fighters who had been operating in Iraq joined with other groups to form the Islamic State in Iraq and Syria (ISIS, sometimes IS or Daesh) and announced the reestablishment of the caliphate, led by a new caliph named Abu Bakr al-Baghdadi. That group found success conquering large sections of territory in Iraq and Syria. The Islamic State maintained control of those areas for a few years until the Iraqi and Syrian governments and their allies reclaimed much of their lost land.

Syria

Hafez al-Assad (1930–2000) was a secular military leader who seized power in 1970 and ruled Syria for decades. As a young man, he was wounded in an assassination attempt by the Muslim Brotherhood, and as a result he maintained deep antipathy toward Islamists for the rest of his life. When the Brotherhood instigated a revolution against him in the city of Hama in 1982, he responded by destroying much of the city and killing somewhere between ten thousand and thirty thousand people.

Assad was an Alawite. Alawites are an off-shoot from Shiism found mostly in western Syria. Because of their esoteric beliefs, neither the Sunnis nor the Shia have been eager to consider them Muslims, but they are traditionally associated with Shiism. Alawites make up about 11 percent of Syria's population, so Assad was a member of a minority Shia ethnic-religious group ruling a country made up mostly of Sunnis. To protect his rule, he placed many Alawites in positions of power, a good portion of whom were his relatives.

Assad ran an efficient police state and stayed in power until his death of natural causes. In the years following the massacre in Hama, he gradually learned how to deal with Muslim leaders. Instead of fighting them, he bought their cooperation through allowing mosques to be built and

A large banner at the entrance of the main market in Damascus in 2006, depicting Bashar al-Assad, Syria's president. The words on the banner are "Syria, God is its Protector."

by making similar concessions. When he died, he was succeeded by his son Bashar.

A few months after the fall of Mubarak's government in Egypt, the Arab Spring arrived in Syria, and protesters demonstrated against the government in several cities. Bashar al-Assad's response was quick and harsh. News reports soon told of brutal reprisals by the Syrian military, which included the bombing of civilian targets. As with the Arab Spring protests elsewhere, Syria's uprising was a popular movement not particularly associated with religion. As the protests turned more violent and clashes evolved into a civil war, however, some of the militia groups that were involved took on an Islamist character that changed the nature of the conflict. Soon Syria was hosting multiple civil conflicts that included groups fighting the government and also secular and Islamist revolutionary groups fighting each other. Turkey, Syria's neighbor to the north, wanted to weaken its regional rival, so it did not prevent people from other countries from entering Syria to join the battles. Those, however, were not Syrian freedom fighters but Islamist jihadis from many countries who traveled there to join ISIS in support of the new caliphate. The idea of a restored caliphate had enormous appeal for many Muslims, and thousands of young men and women moved to Syria to join in the struggle. The Islamic State overpowered most of its rivals and took over significant portions of Syria and Iraq.

Because of the Alawites' historic connection to Shiism, the Sunni-Shia nature of the conflict soon became an important religious element. Iranian advisors and soldiers came to Syria with tons of military supplies to support Assad's government. The Lebanese Shia Islamist group Hezbollah, with its well-trained and well-supplied army, also joined the war on Assad's side.

Turkey

The Ottoman Empire was an explicitly Islamic empire. It was the possessor and guardian of Islam's most important places, and its sultan was the caliph of Islam. When the empire died during World War I, the symbols that made it the center of the Islamic world died with it.

In the aftermath of the war, Mustafa Kemal, an Ottoman general, set out to hold together the Turkish-speaking part of the empire and create a new country out of it. That new country would be the Republic of Turkey. Kemal is better known by his honorary title *Atatürk*, "Father of the Turks." Unlike its Ottoman predecessor, the new Republic of Turkey would be an explicitly *non-*Islamic nation. Atatürk believed that religion was an impediment to progress, so rather than looking in the direction of Islam, he looked toward the West in order to create a secular Western country. His government abolished the position of caliph, removed Sharia from Turkish law and

Mustafa Kemal Atatürk, founder of the Republic of Turkey.

replaced it with secular law based on European models, outlawed the Sufi lodges, made Turkish the language of the *salat*, removed religious schools and replaced them with secular schools, outlawed polygamy, and gave greater rights to women. He placed restrictions on the construction of mosques, put mosques under government control, adopted the European work week, and discarded the Arabic alphabet for the Turkish language, replacing it with the Roman alphabet. It became illegal to wear *hijab* in government buildings and universities.

Atatürk did not make it illegal to be religious, but he and his successors made it difficult for religious people to prosper in society, in education, or in politics.

Since Atatürk's time, Turkey has experienced an ongoing tension between secularization on the one hand and Islam on the other. It has become a modern state that looks more like Europe than like the Middle East, but its road to modernity has been a rocky one. Many Turks still hold to

Atatürk's secular vision for the country, but there are others who span the spectrum from outright Islamists to those who believe that Islam can have a powerful role in a nation whose institutions are secular.

The case of Turgut Özal is one of many that could be mentioned to illustrate how Turkey's competing secular and Islamic instincts have intersected to make the country what it is today. Özal was Turkey's prime minister from 1983 to 1989. He was well educated, but he was also religious. During his university years, he was a secret believer, yet he and his brother found ways to pray privately and unnoticed on campus. His brother went on a trip to the United States and came into contact with Latter-day Saints in Utah. From them he learned that one can be both progressive and religious at the same time—something that contradicted a core message of the Turkish state. His prime minister brother, Turgut, loosened anti-Islamic restrictions as he also instituted modernizing policies that helped in Turkey's economic progress.

In 1995 an Islamist party won the national election, giving Turkey its first Islamist prime minister. The army, in the tradition of Atatürk, was not comfortable with Islamists in power, and two years later the generals forced the prime minister and his government to resign. In 2002 a more centrist Islamist party came to power. The new prime minister, Recep Tayyip Erdoğan, was initially mostly pragmatic in balancing competing interests, and he presided over a modernization push and an economic boom that gained him the support even of many secular voters. Early in his tenure, he curtailed human rights abuses at the same time he removed many anti-Islamic restrictions. But as time went on, his critics saw him as taking more and more power to himself and removing many of the democratic checks and balances of Turkish politics.

Erdoğan's critics disliked what they called "Ottomania." As part of his program of bringing Islam more to the forefront, he and others sought to rehabilitate the reputation of the Ottoman Empire. In popular culture, Ottoman things became trendy, but the real political appeal for Islamists was that the Ottoman Empire was an Islamic state centered in Turkey, and their focus on it helped erase the memory of the secular history that had come after it.

Nigeria

Muslims make up about half of the people of Nigeria, the most populous country in Africa. The rest are primarily Christians. Never part of the Umayyad or Abbasid caliphates, Nigeria's experience with Islam came mostly in the past five hundred years as Islam spread into areas of Sub-Saharan Africa. The relationship between Muslims and Christians has had its difficulties, but most of Nigeria's recent religious conflict has been between Muslims.

In 2002 a group was organized in northeastern Nigeria that called itself "Group of the People of Sunna for Preaching and Jihad." It is commonly known as "Boko Haram," which means, roughly, "Western Education is Haram"—forbidden. Its founders were strict traditionalists who rejected all Western influences as contrary to Islam, including democratic government. In 2009 they began a war against the Nigerian state, attacking police stations, government buildings, and military installations. The goal was to establish an Islamic state in the northern part of the country, which is primarily Muslim. After the first leader's capture and execution, a man named Abubakar Shekau became the group's leader.

Boko Haram's successes were made possible by a variety of conditions, including corrupt and chaotic government, tribal rivalries, and disparity between Nigeria's elites and the poor. The group was able to draw followers largely from the poor countryside but also from cities. Shekau armed Boko Haram's forces by taking over military posts and amassing weapons, and he financed the group by kidnapping and holding hostages for ransom and by extorting money from local officials. Many of the group's soldiers were kidnapped children who were trained to join Boko Haram's army.

Shekau viewed all Muslims except those who agreed with Boko Haram's teachings to be non-Muslims and apostates, thus making them fair targets for attacks. In this he, and some earlier Islamists as well, reflected the view of the Kharijites from Islam's early centuries. In Nigeria and then in neighboring Niger, Chad, and Cameroon, Boko Haram massacred people in crowded markets, bus stations, and mosques. In addition to its army in the field, much of Boko Haram's work

Image taken from a video posted by Boko Haram in 2014, showing kidnapped Muslim and Christian Nigerian schoolgirls. They are dressed not in their colorful African clothing but in full-length coverings supplied by their captors. In the back left is the flag of ISIS.

was done by suicide bombers, particularly children and women. The death toll was astounding, with tens of thousands dead and two million people displaced as refugees in nearby countries and in other parts of Nigeria.

Boko Haram became headline news throughout the world when its soldiers kidnapped nearly three hundred Muslim and Christian girls from a school and announced that it would sell them into slavery. That was not the only time they engaged in that kind of action. Some of the girls were eventually returned to their homes, but many were married off to Boko Haram fighters and others.

In 2015 Shekau pledged Boko Haram's allegiance to al-Baghdadi and the Islamic State, renaming Boko Haram "The Islamic State in West Africa." The next year, ISIS attempted to replace Shekau with another leader because Shekau was too extreme even for ISIS. He refused to step down, however, which led to two separate groups claiming legitimacy. In the following years, combined forces of West African governments began pushing back with some success against the organization.

Indonesia

Indonesia is over five thousand kilometers long and encompasses about six thousand inhabited islands and thousands of other islands. It includes an astounding diversity of cultures and perhaps two hundred different ethnic groups. By the thirteenth century, some areas were adopting Islam through contact with merchants, through the conversion of rulers and other elites, and through missionary activity undertaken by Sufis. It was centuries after that before Indonesia became, as it is today, the country that has more Muslims in it than any other country in the world. Because Islam spread gradually and without a centralized conquest, the process of Islamization was never uniform, and the diversity that had already been part of the island society carried over into Islam as well. As a result, Indonesia probably has more varieties of Islam than any other country and more tolerance for differing applications of Islam than anywhere else. About 87 percent of Indonesians are Muslims, totaling over two hundred million people, but there are also significant and officially recognized minorities of Christians, Hindus, Buddhists, and Confucians.

The Republic of Indonesia was established after World War II. It has had the same forces at work within its society that we have seen in other countries, with pressure from Islamists at various times to make Sharia the law of the land and with resistance to that idea from others. The country has chosen repeatedly not to be an Islamic state and instead to build pluralism into its national fabric.

A large portion of Indonesia's population has adhered to varieties of Islam that included elements from Hinduism, Buddhism, and native beliefs. That kind of syncretism (the blending of elements between religions) is shocking to many Muslims from other lands, but it is a formula that has worked well for centuries in the lives of millions of ordinary Indonesians. More generally, Indonesian Islam is often described as having "traditionalist" and "modernist" orientations, representing two different approaches to religion. Traditionalists are described as those who adhere to the country's historical pattern of adapting Islam to its unique setting with its influences from other sources. Modernists, in contrast, are those who desire to reform and purify the religion and oppose the non-Islamic influences in it. Both of those orientations are associated with organizations that support their ideas, and both have even been represented by political parties. What they have in common is important: both place high value on Indonesia's pluralism and tolerance, and that kind of vision is what has allowed the country to be one where differing beliefs coexist in relative peace. Unfortunately, however, there have been exceptions.

In 2001 one of the provinces was given special autonomy, and it has moved toward implementing Sharia law. Also, in various parts of the country, there has been violence between Christians and Muslims. There are some in Indonesia who wish to import Wahhabism, with its aversion to anything it considers to be religious innovation. The Salafi movement has followers, and even cells of al-Qaeda and ISIS have surfaced. In 2002, coordinated bombings in the resort town of Bali killed over two hundred people, mostly non-Indonesian vacationers. A local Islamist group was responsible, but the evidence showed that the

Islamic Center Mosque in Mataram on the island of Lombok, Indonesia.

attack was financed by al-Qaeda, and Usama bin Laden broadcast a message that Westerners should expect more of the same. Three of the perpetrators were eventually executed.

For the most part, Indonesia has successfully negotiated a variety of religious tensions to be a moderate democratic nation. In its political system, there are several Islamically oriented parties, but they are not among the largest parties in the national parliament, and most of them support the idea of Indonesia as a pluralistic society.

Muslim Nations and the Future

This survey is not intended to paint a gloomy picture of life in Muslim-majority nations. It is important, however, to understand how the intersection of Islam with other political and societal forces has contributed to today's world events. Left out are important countries and many issues of significance, such as relations between Sunnis and Shia in Pakistan, relations between Hindus and Muslims in India, and the religious identities of Lebanon.

It is not easy to predict what the future will hold for countries with large Muslim populations. There is little that is inevitable in this story except that historians and political scientists a generation from now will still have much to write about. One trend that can be observed is that for now, the sense of Islamic identity that Muslims feel is not diminishing. Because of that, it seems likely that many Muslims—even those who are profoundly in favor of free elections and democratic institutions—will nonetheless want to maintain a place for Islam within those institutions. Secularists will want government to be entirely free of religious influence, and Islamists, for their part, will continue to seek a world governed by the principles of Islam.

Chapter 15

Muslims in Europe

Terms and Names to Know

Turks, Battle of Manzikert, Ottoman Empire, Mehmet the Conqueror, Salman Rushdie, Danish cartoonists controversy

In chapter 3 we were introduced to the conquests by Muslim armies after the time of Muhammad. Islam's first encounters with Europeans were part of that process. During the time of the caliphs Umar and Uthman, Arab armies began overtaking the Middle Eastern domains of the Eastern Roman (Byzantine) Empire and soon gained more or less permanent control over all of that empire's territory south of Anatolia (modern-day Turkey). In the 670s, Muslims under the Umayyad caliph Muawiya besieged Constantinople, the Byzantine capital and Europe's greatest city. The Christians were able to repel the attack, but forever after that they were on the defensive and under frequent threat of Muslim invasion.

Medieval Western Europe and the Islamic World

An Umayyad army conquered Spain in the seventh century. Muslims ruled there in the following centuries and were not entirely removed by Christian forces until 1492. Spain was a center of great learning in those centuries, with Muslims making important advances in science, theology, and philosophy.

Europeans also came in contact with Islam through the Crusades. The centuries-long attempt by Western European armies to conquer Palestine and return it to Christianity was ultimately a futile exercise, but the Crusades established permanent connections between the two cultures and opened channels of trade and the transmission of ideas. Europeans as far away as Britain were thus made aware of Islam and the Muslim people.

The Ottoman Empire and Europe

A large group of Turkish-speaking people converted to Islam in their Central Asian homeland in the tenth century. They migrated toward the west and south in the eleventh century and conquered much of Persia and Mesopotamia, even taking control of Baghdad, capital of the Abbasid empire, and conquering Jerusalem. Crossing the eastern frontier of the Byzantine Empire into Anatolia, a Turkish army defeated a large Byzantine force in the Battle of Manzikert in 1071. With the Byzantines no longer able to defend the eastern part of their empire, Turks flowed in. Over the coming decades, they gained control of most of Anatolia. Through assimilation and intermarriage, Islam and the Turkish language became dominant, and most of the area we now call Turkey became Turkish.

By about 1300, a Turkish dynasty in northwestern Anatolia, the Ottomans, had become prominent and powerful. In the coming years, they conquered Anatolia and much of the rest of the Middle East. Motivated by a belief in Islam's supremacy and a desire to gain political power in other lands, they crossed into Europe and conquered much of Greece and a good portion of the Balkans north of Greece. After multiple Muslim attempts since the days of Muawiya, in 1453 Sultan Mehmet II (the Conqueror) took Constantinople and made it his capital. Though it spanned three continents, the Ottoman Empire was now headquartered in Europe in what had been the capital of Eastern Christianity. Conquests continued in Christian lands, and by the end of the fifteenth century most of southeastern Europe from the Black Sea to the Adriatic Sea was in Muslim hands. Moving deep into Europe, the Ottomans

The Hagia Sophia in Istanbul. Constructed in the sixth century at the direction of the Roman emperor Justinian, it was the largest Christian church in the world for over a thousand years. In 1453 the Ottoman sultan Mehmet the Conqueror captured Constantinople. When the *shahada* was pronounced from Hagia Sophia's pulpit and Mehmet and his entourage performed the *salat* in the building, it became a mosque. In later years, the Ottomans built the four surrounding minarets. Hagia Sophia remained a mosque until 1935, when Atatürk declared it a museum and prohibited any kind of worship in it.

threatened Vienna in 1529 and 1683 but failed to conquer it both times.

The Ottoman conquest of the Balkans had lasting consequences because in some areas local people converted to Islam. Today, as a result, Bosnia and Herzegovina, Albania, and Kosovo are Muslim-majority countries, and there are sizable Muslim minorities in Macedonia, Montenegro, and Bulgaria. The followers of Islam in those areas today are not newcomers but indigenous European Muslims, like their ancestors going back many generations.

From their capital, now called Istanbul, the Ottoman sultans were able to rule a huge empire for over half a millennium—remarkably with the same dynasty in power the entire time. Through conquest and trade, they became very prosperous. The Crusades and other contacts had created in Western Europe a taste for Asian commodities like silk and spices, and the Ottomans controlled the trade routes between Europe and South and Central Asia and were enriched from the flow of goods.

As time went on, however, the empire's ability to expand diminished, as did its ability to control its distant domains. The government became increasingly bloated, top heavy, and inefficient.

Colonialism

By the early 1600s, the Ottoman Empire was already on a path of terminal decline, though it would take three more centuries for it to come to an end. In the fifteenth century, Europeans had developed oceangoing ships that were able to sail around Africa and thus bypass routes through the Ottoman Empire to transport goods between Asia and Europe. That was an enormous blow to the Ottoman revenue stream. Europeans sailed across the globe finding new markets in lands that were previously unknown to them, and now the profits from trade flowed to Europe instead of to Istanbul.

Ottoman society and the Ottoman state bureaucracy resisted progress. For example, printing was invented in Western Europe in the mid-1400s, and by the end of that century two million books had been printed in Europe. As a result, literacy spread beyond any previous level in world history, and ideas began to circulate among all classes of people. By comparison, three hundred years later, there were still only a handful of printing presses in the vast Ottoman Empire. By 1920 fewer than 10 percent of Turks could read, while the figure was 92 percent in France and 94 percent in the United States.

The circumstances in Persia were not much different, as the Muslim Safavid state and its successors declined just like the Ottomans. The Muslim world had been displaced by Europe in almost every way—in economic well-being, learning, culture, social organization, technology, and military strength.

Europe took advantage of the decline in the Persian and Turkish Empires. Even before the final dissolution of those empires, their lands were divided up among the European powers into spheres of influence that allowed Europeans to exercise considerable control over the economies of the Middle East and South Asia for their own profit. Much of the Ottoman Empire was in a semicolonial state by the end of the 1800s, as was Persia, but the European nations also had colonies that they ruled outright. Examples include Indonesia, which was ruled by the Netherlands from the eighteenth century to 1949; the Indian subcontinent (now Pakistan, India, and Bangladesh), which was ruled by Great Britain from the eighteenth century to 1947; and Tunisia and Algeria, which were ruled by France from the nineteenth century until 1956 and 1962. At various times, every country in North Africa, South Asia, and the Middle East (with the exception of Saudi Arabia) came under European colonial control. The same was true with the Muslim areas in Central Asia, which were taken over by the Russian Empire and later the Soviet Union.

Immigrants

There are now over twenty-five million Muslims in Europe west of Russia. They are mostly immigrants and children of immigrants from Africa, the Middle East, and South Asia. A Pew Research Center study in 2016 set the number of Muslims at about 4.9 percent of the European population, with over 8 percent in France and Sweden.

The stories of the immigrants are all individual ones, each circumstance being unique, and it is important to emphasize that not all who are identified as Muslims practice their religion. As a pattern, many cease to be observant when they emigrate from Muslim-majority areas, but others become more observant in their new settings than they were in their home countries. Some general observations will help us see the big picture of why so many Muslims now call Europe their home and how well they are doing there.

Colonialism provided one of the earliest channels for the migration of Muslims to Europe. In the examples above, the connections between European countries and their colonies led to the early migration of people from Indonesia, India, and North Africa into the Netherlands, Britain, and France. Their motives included education, work, and better economic opportunities.

By the last third of the twentieth century, the pace of immigration into Europe had increased dramatically from previous decades, and the destinations were no longer tied so closely to the colonial past. Some European countries experienced labor shortages beginning in the 1960s, and they imported workers from other countries. Morocco became a source of many guest workers, notably for mining jobs in Belgium. Germany imported thousands of Turkish guest workers, who often sent their earnings home to support their families. Initially most of those workers returned to their homes in Turkey, but in time many decided to stay. Because the government and many Germans considered them only temporary, there was much resistance to their staying, but courts eventually ruled that they could remain in Germany. Children born there of Turkish parents did not receive German citizenship until a law made that possible in 2000, but those children still had problems in Germany if they wanted to have Turkish citizenship as well. Germany now has about five million Muslims, about two-thirds of whom are Turks.

European universities became magnets for many people from Muslim countries. In many instances, graduates became comfortable in their new environments and opted to stay, often because they knew that job prospects in their home countries were limited, and Europe provided opportunities.

It is often said that the experience of immigrants to Europe differs from that of most who have moved to the United States. In general, it appears that Muslims have assimilated more successfully in the United States than in Europe. In Europe, a significant number of Muslims live in areas that are largely inhabited by fellow Muslims, where they are able to keep their ancestral languages alive and reproduce much of their familiar cultures. One reason for this is that so many immigrants migrate to Europe for blue-collar,

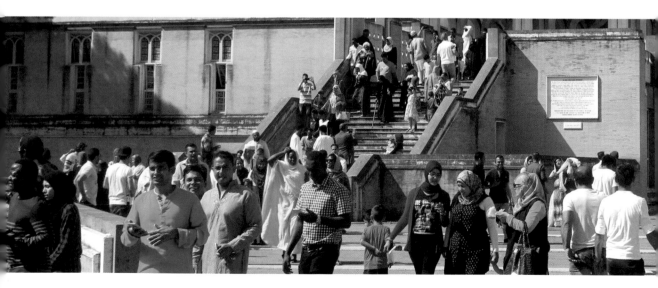

Worshippers at the Mosque of Rome, the largest mosque in Western Europe. This mosque serves worshippers who have immigrated to Italy from many countries in Africa, the Middle East, and Asia. In contrast, Europe also has mosques that serve mostly single-country, or single-ethnic-group, immigrant communities.

low-skilled jobs and live close to their places of employment. In addition, many immigrate to areas where they have relatives or already know people from home. In America, some areas have been magnets for Muslim immigrants, but the majority of Muslims in the United States have no immediate Muslim neighbors. Instead, they live—as members of other faith groups do—interspersed among the general population. As a result, most American Muslim children have been quickly acculturated into American society. Most second- and third-generation Muslim Americans are not fluent in the native languages of their parents and grandparents, and they view themselves as Americans.

The economic circumstances of Muslims in Europe and the United States are also different. Muslim immigrants to America are generally better educated than their European counterparts, and they and their children are better educated than the US population in general. The income of Muslims in the United States is about at the US average. Muslims in Europe are less educated than the general population and considerably less prosperous. These disparities have contributed to difficulties in integration into the established societies.

Of course, there are many exceptions, but so far it seems that the melting-pot metaphor applies more in the United States than in Europe.

Challenges

In 1988 a British author named Salman Rushdie wrote a novel that many viewed as disrespectful of Muhammad and Islam. It caused an international uproar. The supreme leader of Iran, Ayatollah Khomeini, issued a *fatwa* against Rushdie that called upon Muslims to execute him wherever he could be found. The British had to provide protection for Rushdie because his life was in danger, and anti-Western demonstrations and riots broke out in several countries. When Mohammed Khatami was Iran's president, he stated that the *fatwa* with its death sentence was void, but supreme leader Ali Khamenei reaffirmed it. Rushdie eventually moved to the United States.

We saw on page 5 that Muslims are very sensitive about the issue of depicting Muhammad. Europe's relationship with Islam was tested in 2005 when Danish editorial cartoonists published

cartoons depicting Muhammad in unflattering ways and showing Muslims as terrorists. The purpose of the artists was to make a knowingly controversial statement in favor of the Western values of freedom of expression and a free press. Violence broke out in several cities, including in Europe, and innocent people died as a result. Ten years later, some French Muslims murdered several people in the office of a magazine that had published satirical depictions of Muhammad.

These freedom-of-expression issues are historically important because they caused some Europeans to question whether Islam is able to function in free, democratic societies: Can a British citizen not write things in a book that Muslims do not like? And can journalists not print what they want? Questions like these tested the feelings of some Europeans toward their immigrant Muslim neighbors.

Terrorism has hit Europe very hard, with deadly attacks from al-Qaeda and then from ISIS, often perpetrated by European Muslims. Some countries have banned headscarves in schools and veiled faces in public, raising sensitivities that may seem unimportant to some but that are of great significance to many Muslims. Muslims have also experienced difficulties regarding the building and design of mosques.

A small mosque in Louvain-la-Neuve, Belgium, lacks a minaret and other features that would identify it from a distance as a mosque. The building of mosques has sometimes been a sensitive political issue in Europe. Mosque designs reflect not only Islamic tradition but sometimes also local customs and cultural concerns. This mosque was designed deliberately to fit in with its environment and not look foreign or exotic.

Many Europeans were surprised to learn that among those who flocked to Syria and Iraq to join ISIS were thousands of Europeans—young Muslims who had grown up in Europe as well as more recent immigrants. Those included women as well as men, and they included many who had never been particularly observant Muslims. Research into the motivations of the recruits showed that joining ISIS gave them the feeling that they were taking part in an important cause that would be of benefit to the world—the reestablishment of the caliphate. Underlying causes have been attributed to anti-Islamic rhetoric in Europe, economic disadvantage, and a lack of integration into European societies. As we saw in chapter 12, the vast majority of European Muslims, like those in other countries, reject any form of terrorism or violence against innocents and desire to live in their countries in peace and in harmony with others.

In the 2010s, as a result of political turmoil in the Middle East and Africa, millions of Muslims fled their homelands and sought asylum in other countries. These were not immigrants but refugees—refugees from disastrous situations such as the wars in Syria and Iraq. They often brought nothing with them but their families. Most (but not all) European countries, recognizing that this was a humanitarian catastrophe, provided a safe haven and, for the most part, showed remarkable kindness and generosity. In due time, there was resistance from nationalists and others who wondered if the resources were available to embrace so many displaced people and what their presence would mean for Europe's future. Many Americans—whose own government was less welcoming of the refugees—applauded the efforts of the European leaders.

Europeans know that examples like these show that there is work to be done with respect to Europe's Muslim populations. These are significant issues, but it is important not to focus only on the challenges. Muslim immigrants have moved to Europe for the advantages that come from living in societies that value freedom and provide economic opportunity. They stay because they know that their lives are likely to be more secure and prosperous in Europe than in their homelands, and they want their children and grandchildren to grow up there as European Muslims.

Muslims can be found in Europe in every walk of life and in every trade and profession, contributing like other members of society. They are neighbors and coworkers of other Europeans. Perhaps most important of all for the future, indigenous European children are growing up with Muslim classmates and friends. Indeed, despite difficulties, most European Muslims are succeeding, and they are steadily becoming an important part of the European social landscape. One evidence for this is that in 2016 the citizens of London elected a practicing Muslim as mayor, a man who had served several years in Parliament before that. He was not the first Muslim mayor in the United Kingdom, as there had already been others, but it was significant that Londoners felt comfortable bringing a Muslim to such an important political position. Britain had long had many Muslim citizens, most of whom were integrated and doing well. The fact that there was a Muslim candidate, though a major topic of conversation in the campaign, apparently did not hurt him significantly in the election.

Chapter 16

Muslims in North America

Terms and Names to Know

Wallace D. Fard, Nation of Islam, Elijah Muhammad, Muhammad Ali, Malcolm X

Muslims were present in North America from the beginning of European exploration and colonization. The first in the New World probably came from Spain and Portugal with the earliest European conquerors. The first to settle in what would later be the United States came on slave ships. It is estimated that as many as 10–20 percent of enslaved Africans brought to America were Muslims, though we will never know with certainty. The first recorded accounts of Islamic worship in North America come from whites who observed enslaved people bowing together. Pockets of practicing enslaved Muslims appear to have lasted for decades, but the descendants of most of them eventually became Christians.

Immigrants

The majority of Muslims in the United States and Canada are first- or second-generation immigrants from other countries. They come from the Middle East, Africa, and South Asia—areas of the world that have the largest Muslim populations. They come for the same reasons that have motivated millions of others to make the same journey—a quest for freedom and economic opportunity. On pages 93 and 94, we were already introduced to Muslim immigration to America as it compares to immigration to Europe.

Many immigrants to North America arrived from Ottoman lands in the late nineteenth century, followed by others from the same area in the early twentieth century. A common experience for many of them was that they or their children intermarried with other North Americans and assimilated into the common culture. A typical example is that of the Aziz family we met in chapter 11. None of the children in the family ended up as practicing Muslims; most converted to Christianity and married Christians. The descendants of many early immigrants lost their Islamic identity, and thus there are thousands of white Canadians and Americans who do not know that some of their ancestors were Muslims.

The Mile High Islamic Center in Denver, Colorado, USA (above), was originally a Baptist church. It was modified extensively to house a congregation of Serbian Muslims, most of whom have immigrated to America since the 1990s. The Shia mosque in Taylorsville, Utah, USA—the al-Rasool Islamic Center (below)—is a converted century-old Latter-day Saint church. These are typical of many buildings in North America that have been converted into mosques. As immigrant Muslim communities become more prosperous, they are able to construct new purpose-built mosques. Examples can be seen on pages ix and 41.

In following this pattern, those immigrants were doing what most others of the time were doing, becoming part of the melting pot.

By the late 1960s the pattern was changing. There were more immigrants from Muslim nations, and the pace of assimilation slowed down. That new wave of immigrants brought with it a clearer sense of Islamic identity, and unlike their predecessors many of them maintained it by building mosques, cultural centers, and Islamic schools.

The Utah Valley Islamic Center, Orem, Utah, USA, in 2018. Many young Muslim communities rent space for worship in commercial properties. As this local community grew out of its rented space, it was able to buy this house and convert it into a mosque while raising funds to build a new and larger facility.

Muslim immigrants in the past few decades seem more determined than any previous generation to preserve their identity as Muslims. Not all of their children and grandchildren will feel the same way, and so in this also they will likely reflect the experience of many other immigrant communities. An Arab immigrant from about fifty years ago told me that as many as 80 percent of immigrant Muslims he had known eventually ceased to be observant. The imam of a Bosnian mosque told me that of four thousand Bosnian Muslims in his area, his congregation includes only three hundred families. He lamented that a large percentage of the children of immigrants in his community were marrying non-Muslims. Despite these realities, the continuing influx of Muslims and the persistence of those who remain observant will assure that the Muslim population in North America will keep growing.

Muslims believe in a worldwide united *umma*, and they consider all Muslims (excluding the Shia, for some Sunnis) to be their brothers and sisters. But most live in Muslim-majority national settings where they are most comfortable among people like themselves. Pakistanis are accustomed to worshiping with Pakistanis, Arabs with Arabs, and especially Shia with fellow Shia. History has shown that newly arrived immigrants often segregate along national or sectarian lines. Thus large North American cities with established Muslim populations often have nationality-based mosques alongside congregations that reflect a mix of ethnic, racial, and national differences. Subsequent generations, however, show increased assimilation.

A Shia immigrant from Iraq in a midsize American city told me that when he moved there in the 1970s, he and his fellow Shia first met with Sunnis. But as soon as they could afford it, they split from that congregation so they could have their own mosque. In that same city, there are now two mosques that cater to Somalis, another one for Bosnians (the Turks worship with the Bosnians because they feel more comfortable with the European Bosnians than with anyone else), and some larger international mosques for most everyone else, including Arabs and immigrants from South Asia (mostly from Pakistan, India, and Bangladesh). An African American friend, wanting to visit and worship in that city, was discouraged by the options and wrote to me, asking, "Isn't there an *indigenous* mosque there?" Larger cities have more Muslims and more options.

A Pakistani immigrant told me of his experience in the United States. He and other immigrants chose to attend a mosque where the imam spoke English with an American accent. This was important, he said, because American English (as opposed to English with a British, Indian, Somali, or Arab accent) is the common language of that diverse community. It is the one variety of English that all of them could understand. This man told me that his sons were "very American" boys. They attended a public school and acted very much like other young Americans. Yet they also went to the mosque each Sunday for religion classes so they could learn the Qur'an.

The First Mosques in North America

Recall that the word *mosque* means "bowing-down place," and thus a mosque does not need to be a building but a location with a border to set it apart from the outside world. The first American mosques were thus likely the places in woods or fields that enslaved Africans prepared so they could come together to perform the *salat*.

There is evidence that in the early 1900s, Muslim immigrants to cities in the eastern United States rented halls to serve as mosques. The earliest-known building constructed in the United States specifically to be a mosque was in the Detroit

Built in 1921, the first mosque constructed in the United States, Highland Park, Michigan.

suburb of Highland Park, Michigan. In 1921 a mosque was built there to meet the needs of the Muslim immigrant community that was growing with the automobile industry. Within the decade

This mosque in Cedar Rapids, Iowa, built in 1936, is the oldest mosque still standing in the United States and thus has the honor of calling itself the "Mother Mosque of America."

that building was sold and used for other purposes, but soon other mosques began to be built in that city and elsewhere as Muslims arrived in North America and organized into worship communities. The oldest mosque still standing in the United States, built in 1936, is in Cedar Rapids, Iowa, and the first mosque built in Canada, constructed in 1938, is in Edmonton, Alberta. These buildings show that Islam was not restricted to big coastal cities but could be found in many locations as immigrants sought places to build homes and raise families in their new countries.

African American Muslims

In the early decades of the twentieth century, there were several Islam-related organizations in the United States that catered primarily to African Americans. Those ranged from groups with questionable Islamic connections (such as the Moorish

Science Temple) to groups based on unorthodox Muslim traditions (such as the Ahmadiyya) to groups that were more political than religious. Often called collectively "Black Muslims," what those groups had in common was that they appealed to the need of many African Americans to have a sense of pride in their heritage and a connection with their pre-slavery roots. Most of those groups did not succeed in terms of flourishing to the present time, but their importance is that they became a very significant conduit for many into mainstream Islam.

About 1930 a man in Detroit named Wallace D. Fard started a religious organization for African Americans called the "Lost-Found Nation of Islam in the Wilderness of North America." Originally from New Zealand, Fard claimed to be from Mecca. His message was that Africans living in America were displaced, lost in the wilderness of a foreign land, and needed to reclaim their true identity as Muslims. Fard disappeared in 1934, after which the organization was run by one of his converts, Elijah Muhammad (1897–1975). Fard's history is so obscure that it is difficult to tell how much of the organization's belief system came from him and how much was the product of Elijah Muhammad.

The Nation of Islam is one of America's most fascinating religious stories. More than being considered an offshoot of Islam, it can best be described as a uniquely American religion that reflects the time and place where it came into being. Its Islamic connections are interesting, but its connection with America's racial history is much more important.

The religious component of the Nation of Islam shows why Muslims in general, especially outside North America, have never seen it as Islamic in any real way. The Nation taught that Wallace D. Fard was Allah and that Elijah Muhammad was a prophet. Things that are most characteristically Islamic were missing from the Nation, such as the *salat*, use of the Qur'an and the *hadith* literature, and the Hajj. In the place of mosques with open floors, the Nation had large meeting halls filled with chairs that served as the site of sermons and teaching.

The political component of the Nation is a product of its historical narrative: All people were originally black, and all American blacks descended from Muslims. White people are an aberration. They are devils and enemies. The oppression black people have suffered from whites is evidence that whites are perverse by nature, and no accommodation with them will succeed. Thus Elijah Muhammad and his followers argued for peaceful coexistence with whites but not for integration.

The Nation of Islam's strong social component received less attention in the public press, but it has had the most lasting impact. Elijah Muhammad placed great emphasis on things he believed would strengthen the African American community, such as education and economic development. Many of society's ills, such as prostitution, crime, and substance abuse, were tools that the white oppressors had used to keep black people down. Society in general would not help blacks, nor should blacks want it to, but on their own they needed to achieve moral progress, develop strong two-parent families, separate themselves from adultery, fornication, crime, and other evils of society, and abstain completely from alcohol and drugs. It was probably this part of the message, more than any other, that attracted thousands of African Americans, primarily in northern US cities, to join the Nation.

In the 1960s the most high-profile convert was Cassius Clay (1942–2016), a young professional boxer. After he won the heavyweight championship of the world, he revealed that he was a member of the Nation of Islam. Elijah Muhammad gave him the name Muhammad Ali. As an athlete and a social commentator, Ali was a polarizing figure, but through his boxing he became perhaps the most well-known person in the world, and his devotion to Elijah Muhammad's teachings gave the Nation enormous credibility among African Americans.

At about the same time, Malcolm X (1925–65) became the face that most white Americans associated with the Nation. He was an extraordinary public speaker who advocated anger, resistance, and revolution in the effort of black Americans to achieve their civil rights. It was common at the time to contrast his approach with that of Martin Luther King Jr., a Christian pastor who advocated nonviolence. Malcolm had been converted to the Nation of Islam while in prison. When he was released, he sought out Elijah Muhammad,

Muhammad Ali, upper left in the black suit, listens to the preaching of Elijah Muhammad.

who recognized his talents and gave him important positions in the organization. For over a decade, he was a tireless worker who advocated the Nation's cause on television and in public speeches. His strident tone caused many white Americans to take notice.

By 1964 Malcolm had come to believe that Elijah Muhammad was corrupt because he discovered that he had several mistresses. Malcolm withdrew from the Nation, and shortly thereafter he converted to Sunni Islam. He went on the Hajj to Mecca and found people of all races worshipping together, including white people. What he saw there confirmed his thoughts that the Nation's core teachings regarding racial identities were wrong. When he returned to the United States, he started a Sunni mosque in New York, and in 1965 he was murdered by members of the Nation of Islam.

When Elijah Muhammad died in 1975, his son Wallace D. Muhammad succeeded him as

Malcolm X in 1964.

leader of the Nation. Wallace soon dissolved the organization and transitioned with most of his followers to Sunnism. Not long thereafter, one of Elijah Muhammad's most outspoken supporters, Louis Farrakhan, created a new organization that he described as a resurrection of the Nation with its original teachings. He continued the emphasis on economic development and moral progress, but he became a controversial public figure, and he and his organization were accused of being anti-American, racist, and anti-Semitic.

Many former members of Elijah Muhammad's Nation of Islam eventually became Sunnis, leaving behind his racial ideology and esoteric beliefs and embracing genuine Islam. Among those was Muhammad Ali, who went on the Hajj in the 1970s and again over a decade later. Over the following years, Ali represented Islam very positively to his admirers around the world, and in the United States he became to many the face of American Islam. Others of Elijah Muhammad's followers went back to Christianity, but American Christianity's role as accomplice (or at least bystander) in slavery, segregation, and racial discrimination made it a less-desirable destination for people who had felt empowered by Malcolm X's message of black self-determination. For all

its ideas that were not Islamic at all, the Nation became the means by which tens of thousands of African Americans became Muslims.

Muslim organizations have been very active in prison ministries in an effort to promote Islam and improve the lives of African Americans who have made unwise choices. Islam's emphasis on living without drugs, alcohol, crime, and promiscuity has led many prisoners to conversion as well as to more productive lives. In addition, even though only a minority of slave-immigrant Africans were Muslims, many African Americans feel that in joining Islam, they are reconnecting with their roots. For the same reason, it is not unheard of for even non-Muslim American blacks to have Islamic names.

Worshippers at mosques in the United States that attract mostly nonimmigrants are in large measure convert African Americans, but not exclusively so. People of all races have converted and joined the Muslim communities. American converts, however, are not nearly as numerous as the Muslims who have immigrated in recent decades from other lands, whose children and grandchildren will likely compose the majority for many years to come.

Conclusion

Who Is a Muslim?

Once I asked an immigrant to Canada if he were a Muslim. He replied in the affirmative. I then asked him, "Do you go to the mosque?" He laughed as though I had asked a stupid question, and then he said, "No!" I decided to continue the same test, and over the next few days I asked several other Arab and Iranian immigrants. The answer was always the same. In Muslim-majority countries I have asked the same questions, but I have observed that fewer people in those lands are comfortable saying that they don't go to the mosque, even if they never do.

Non-Muslims are often surprised to learn that not all Muslims attend the mosque or pray five times a day, despite the injunctions in the Qur'an and the *hadith*. Muslims, like adherents of other faiths, come in all varieties of observance. Many are more inclined to go to the mosque for Friday prayers than at any other time of the week, and many more attend on holy days more than on other occasions—a phenomenon not unknown from other religions.

What the vast majority of nonattenders have in common is that they still identify themselves as Muslims. Recent polls, in fact, indicate that far more American Muslims say their religion is important to them than pray daily or attend a mosque weekly. Their Muslim identity is a separate matter from their level of involvement, and even though they don't participate in the religion, they still choose to feel connected to it. This is not surprising, because Islam, in addition to being a religious system, is a broad-ranging culture that impacts all facets of life.

Being a Muslim

In the early centuries of Islam, the question "Who is a Muslim?" was a real one that had important implications. The issue arose in the seventh century when the Kharijites that we met in chapter 3, wanting to purify the *umma*, decided that many people were not Islamic enough and declared them to be non-Muslims. This brought up some

Muslims: American high school track stars in *hijab* (left); Palestinian kindergartners visiting the Dome of the Rock in Jerusalem (above); Syrian children walking home from school (above right); and a class of young Americans from an Islamic school (below right).

questions: Can someone be expelled from the *umma* for bad behavior? If so, who gets to decide whether someone is not Islamic enough to be called a Muslim? Is being a Muslim a matter of doing certain things or a matter of identifying oneself as a Muslim? Related to these is another question: Can we judge from a Muslim's behavior whether he will go to heaven or to hell?

The Kharijite answer to this last question was yes, but as in most cases like this, the consensus was the more moderate position. *Self-identifying*, rather than *doing*, became the feature that proved people to be Muslims. Most agreed that if someone calls herself a Muslim she is one, and we are not in a position to judge where she will end up in eternity, no matter what she does. Not everyone has been happy with this conclusion, so it is still being discussed today.

This approach has some drawbacks. After a particularly egregious terrorist attack, an American Muslim woman said, "Why do *we* have to keep apologizing for things like this? *They're not us!*" Islamic advocacy groups, Muslims, and friends of Muslims sometimes find themselves having to respond to misdeeds committed in the name of Islam that violate the principles that most Muslims seek to uphold. It has not been an easy task for them to convince people who watch European and North American television that "They're not us."

Some years ago I was the moderator of a panel of American Muslims on the topic of Islam's public image in the United States. All of the panelists expressed frustration at how their people and religion were depicted in the media. Some blamed the media itself, which had been a common response from many Muslims for a long time. Those who really know Islamic countries know that news reports from them are often exaggerated or inaccurately biased. Muslims have been over-represented as villains in movies and on television, and because they are not well known in the West, it has been easy for some to dehumanize them and view them as "the Other." "Islamophobia," at its root, means "fear of Islam." But in practice it suggests a disliking of Islam that can lead to prejudicial feelings and actions against Muslims. Seeing the behavior of extremists, many have come to see those extremists as representative of Islam and not as anomalies that the vast majority of Muslims denounce and disclaim. Muslims are well aware of the problem. One prominent Western Muslim stated, "Too often, the people who are 'representing' the Islamic faith aren't representative, they're angry men with beards. And that's not what Islam is about."

In our panel discussion, a nuanced conclusion rose to the surface that placed the burden of accurately representing Islam on Muslims themselves. It went something like this: Muslims must not allow the worst elements among them to become the spokespeople for the rest of them. Following up on that was a second conclusion: Muslims in the West need to do a better job of representing themselves so non-Muslims will better know what Islam is and what Muslims are like. One study showed that knowing a Muslim personally, rather than simply knowing about Islam, did more to foster positive feelings toward the religion than anything else.

There has been much progress, and the coming decades will likely show even more. Muslims are becoming more visible in the West as neighbors, mothers at youth soccer games, doctors, school teachers, classmates, and store clerks. Their seemingly ordinary lives will likely change many minds and make it harder for criminals to be viewed as the norm. It is easy to demonize people we don't know, so perhaps the best thing Muslims in the West can do to change minds is to become known.

As noted in the introduction, this book was written with two objectives in mind: to help its non-Muslim readers interact in a respectful and knowledgeable way with Muslims and to help them become better informed consumers of the news. Its title, *Islam: A First Encounter*, suggests that there are other encounters yet to come. As the visibility of Islam and Muslims continues to grow throughout the world and in our own neighborhoods, understanding them will become increasingly important for the future.

Author and Acknowledgments

Author

Kent P. Jackson, PhD, Near Eastern Studies, University of Michigan, is a retired professor of religion at Brigham Young University in Provo, Utah, USA.

Acknowledgments

This book is published with the assistance of the Religious Studies Center at Brigham Young University, for which I thank Devan Jensen, Brent Nordgren, Shirley Ricks, Petra Javadi-Evans, Megan Judd, and Emily V. Strong. I express thanks to all my Muslim friends, students, and acquaintances over many years who have unknowingly contributed so much to this book through conversations about their lives and experiences. I am grateful to academic friends who have shared their expertise by reading all or parts of the manuscript, offering improvements and steering me to fertile ground for better discussions. These include Bashir Bashir, Chad F. Emmett, William J. Hamblin, James R. Kearl, Quinn Mecham, Samuel P. Nielson, Daniel C. Peterson, and especially Donna Lee Bowen and James A. Toronto. Nancy Jackson deserves unending thanks for reviewing not only this book but everything I've written since 1975.

I express my thanks to the individuals and institutions that made the images in this book possible. The images are courtesy of Bardo Museum, Tunis, page 10; Bibliothèque nationale de France, pages 25, 27; British Museum, London, back cover below right; Batoul and Nour Chouiki and Malden High School, Malden, Massachusetts, page 104 left; Chad F. Emmett, back cover above left, page 89; Kent P. Jackson, front cover, back cover above right, back cover below left, back cover below right, pages v, vii, 1, 8, 9, 10, 11, 13, 14, 15, 19, 21, 22, 23, 29 above, 30, 31 above, 32 above, 32 below, 35, 39, 40, 41, 42, 43 left, 43 right, 44 above, 44 below, 45, 46, 47 above, 47 below left, 47 below right, 49, 52, 53, 54, 55 above, 55 below, 56, 58, 59, 61 above, 61 below, 62, 63, 64, 68 above, 68 below, 71, 75, 83, 85, 90, 91, 96, 97 above, 97 below, 98, 103, 104 right, 105 above, 105 below, 107, 109; Library of Congress, Washington, DC, page 101 above, 101 below; National Archives,

Washington, DC, page 78; Samuel P. Nielson, page 94; Aspen Robins, page 31 below; David M. Whitchurch, page 34; and generous contributors to Wikimedia Commons, pages 3, 4, 5, 24, 29 below, 37, 38, 48, 73, 80, 82, 84, 93, 99 below.

Background images on chapter title pages are as follows: page v, Amr ibn al-As Mosque, Cairo, Egypt; page 1, King Abdullah Mosque, Amman, Jordan; page 8, Abraham's Tomb, Hebron, Palestine; page 15, Umayyad Mosque, Aleppo, Syria; page 22, Haci Özbek Mosque, İznik, Turkey; page 29, Bosniak Mosque Maryam, Salt Lake City, Utah, USA; page 34, al-Aqsa Mosque, Jerusalem, Palestine; page 40, Ulu Cami, Bursa, Turkey; page 46, al-Zaytuna Mosque, Tunis, Tunisia; page 49, Sayyida Ruqayya Mosque, Damascus, Syria; page 54, Ibn Tulun Mosque, Cairo, Egypt; page 63, Nasir Muhammad Mosque, Cairo, Egypt; page 71, Ksar Mosque, Tunis, Tunisia; page 75, Muayyad Mosque, Cairo, Egypt; page 83, Umayyad Mosque, Damascus, Syria; page 90, Küçük Ayasofya Mosque, Istanbul, Turkey; page 96, Masjid Ikhlas, Denver, Colorado, USA; page 103, Mosque for the Praise of Allah, Boston, Massachusetts, USA; page 107, Rüstem Paşa Mosque, Istanbul, Turkey; page 109, al-Rasool Islamic Center, Taylorsville, Utah, USA.

Images on cover: front, Dome of the Rock, Jerusalem; back above left, Agung Mosque, Pacitan, Indonesia; back above right, al-Husayn Mosque, Cairo, Egypt; back below left, Yeni Cami, Istanbul, Turkey; back below right, Mamluk-period mosque lamps.

Index